THE ROMAN HERITAGE:

Textiles from Egypt and the Eastern Mediterranean 300 to 600 AD

THE ROMAN HERITAGE

TEXTILES FROM EGYPT AND THE EASTERN MEDITERRANEAN 300 TO 600 AD

JAMES TRILLING

THE TEXTILE MUSEUM

Washington, D.C. 1982   Volume 21 of "Textile Museum Journal"

Copyright 1982 by the Textile Museum
2320 S Street N.W., Washington, D.C. 20008

Typesetting by VIP Systems, Alexandria, Virginia

Printed by Garamond Pridemark Press, Baltimore, Maryland

Designed by Susan Lehmann, Washington, D.C.

Library of Congress Cataloging in Publication Data

Trilling, James, 1948–
The Roman heritage.
Catalogue of an exhibition.
Issued also as: Textile Museum journal; v. 20.
1. Textiles, Roman—Egypt—Exhibitions. 2. Textiles, Coptic—Exhibitions. 3. Textiles, Roman—Near East—Exhibitions. I. Textile Museum (Washington, D.C.) II. Textile Museum journal; v. 20. III. Title.
NK8988.A1T74   746.39′015′0740153   82-50367
ISBN 0-87405-019-7 (pbk.)   AACR2
ISSN 0083-7407

PREFACE

Between 1925 and his death in 1957, George Hewitt Myers, founder of the Textile Museum, assembled an outstanding collection of Late Roman and medieval textiles of the type widely known as Coptic. Since his death the Museum has added to the collection, and now possesses well over four hundred examples. They range from small fragments to a number of pieces remarkable for their size and completeness, including several that are among the largest and finest known today.

Plans for an exhibition and catalogue of Coptic textiles were first discussed in 1975 with the late Richard Ettinghausen, then Consultative Chairman of the Department of Islamic Art at the Metropolitan Museum, and a long time Trustee of the Textile Museum. In 1977, under a grant from the National Endowment for the Arts, Susan MacMillan Arensberg undertook a technical analysis of many of the Coptic textiles in the Museum's collection, the results of which appear here in the catalogue entries. At the same time Raymond Schwartz began to re-photograph most of the textiles. More recently Clarissa Palmai, Conservator at the Museum, has remounted or has prepared for exhibition for the first time a great number of the pieces. One textile, the great hanging with flying Erotes (cat. no. 1) was remounted by Katrina de Carbonnel under the general direction of Joseph Columbus, Textile Conservator at the National Gallery of Art. Funds for this work were provided by the Charlotte Palmer Phillips Foundation through the interest of my father, Andrew Oliver.

In June 1981 the Museum was fortunate in persuading James Trilling, an historian of Late Roman and Byzantine Art, to join the staff of the Museum and to begin work at once on this catalogue of textiles of the Roman period from Egypt. Partial support for the printing of the catalogue has come from the National Endowment for the Arts, a Federal Agency to which the Textile Museum is deeply indebted.

ANDREW OLIVER, JR.
Director 1975-1981

CONTENTS

5 Preface by ANDREW OLIVER, JR.

9 Acknowledgments

11 Introduction

29 Tapestries

93 Textiles with patterns in weft-loop pile

96 Drawloom textiles in wool and silk (with a structural analysis by Ann Pollard Rowe)

102 Resist-dyed textiles

104 Appendix I: The development of interlace and related patterns

109 Appendix II: Remounting of the tapestry cat. no. 1, by KATRINA DE CARBONNEL

110 Table of Accession and Catalogue Numbers

111 Bibliography

ACKNOWLEDGMENTS

To thank the people who have helped in the preparation of *The Roman Heritage* is to list everyone connected in any way with the Textile Museum. Without the enthusiastic support of the Board of Trustees, the project could never have been undertaken. The entire staff of the Museum made me welcome from the moment of my arrival, and have gone on to meet my requests for assistance, whether of a theoretical or a practical kind, with cheerful efficiency and unfailing patience. Thanks too must go to the volunteers who have made my work so much easier by helping with the round of everyday tasks that such a project entails, and to the docents, who by their stimulating questions reassured me, in moments of doubt, that Late Roman textiles can be more than just a series of puzzles for a few specialists.

There are two people to whom I am especially indebted. The first is Andrew Oliver, Jr., until 1982 Director of the Textile Museum. It was he who first conceived the plan for an exhibition and catalogue of the Museum's Late Roman collection. Although it could not be completed before his departure, the project remains very much his. In addition to providing the initial impetus, he has continued to act as editor for the catalogue, and has counselled me on matters large or small at every stage of its production.

The second person to whom special thanks are due is Susan MacMillan Arensberg, who in 1977 examined many of the Museum's Late Roman textiles. Her work included both technical analysis and art historical research, amounting in effect to a preliminary catalogue of a large part of the collection. In matters of technique, especially, I have relied on her conclusions whenever I could, and when this was not possible have tried to learn from them.

Patricia Fiske, as Acting Director of the Museum, has overseen the printing of the catalogue and the arrangement of the exhibition, providing much-needed advice and support throughout. Ann Pollard Rowe analyzed the structure of the drawloom fabrics, and Mattiebelle Gittinger provided information on the technique of resist-dyeing. Katherine Freshley, the Museum's Librarian, obtained many necessary books and articles with a speed that often seemed magical. Blenda Femenias and Vicki Mavis typed the manuscript, shouldering the burden of an onrushing deadline with unflagging and enspiriting good grace. The greater portion of the photographs are by Raymond Schwartz, who has done consistently splendid work despite a forced-march schedule. Mary Lee Berger-Hughes has sustained me at every point with humor and encouragement.

Clarissa Palmai, the Museum's Conservator, and Cynthia Sapia-Bosch, worked heroically at the exacting task of mounting the textiles for the exhibition. No one who admires the textiles today can fail to appreciate their contribution, for it is thanks to their efforts alone that many of these incredibly fragile relics can be displayed.

Sollie Barnes, Richard Timpson, and Tony Rodriguez are responsible not only for the actual hanging of the exhibition, but long before that, for carrying out a hundred different tasks without which neither the catalogue nor the exhibition could have come into being. Itaka Schlubach also gave invaluable help in the preparation and mounting of the exhibition. My gratitude to them knows no bounds.

Many people outside the Textile Museum have helped me in the preparation of this catalogue. Nobuko Kajitani, Textile Conservator at the Metropolitan Museum of Art, and Edna Russmann, Assistant Curator of Egyptian Art at the same museum, gave generously of their time and expertise. Dr. Geoffrey T. Martin of the Petrie Collection, University College London, supplied important information. Professor Ernst Kitzinger, presently at the Institute for Advanced Study in Princeton, helped me with a particularly difficult problem. David Buckton of the British Museum, and Jacqueline Lafontaine-Dosogne of the Musées Royaux d'Art et d'Histoire, Brussels, generously provided photographs. The staff of the Dumbarton Oaks Center for Byzantine Studies have assisted me in innumerable ways, making it a constant pleasure to use their magnificent research facilities.

Finally, I owe a very special debt of gratitude to my wife Dore. She has shown me that moral support in no way depends on physical proximity, and has kept me going even at a distance of four hundred miles!

INTRODUCTION

The word Coptic is derived from the Greek *Aiguptios*, meaning Egyptian, and is commonly applied to all Greco-Roman or medieval textiles that have been found in Egypt and are not of Islamic origin. I shall avoid using the term, however, because it has implications which limit rather than enhance our appreciation of the textiles' artistic function and their place in the history of design. I shall return to this problem of terminology. For the moment it is enough to point out that as a generic term, "Coptic" does not distinguish between periods or styles. This catalogue, comprising only a portion of the Museum's holdings, focuses on the textile art of the Late Roman Empire, and covers the period approximately from the fourth through the sixth century. Since the term Coptic is applied to many different styles, including some which cannot by any reasonable criterion be called Roman, and is used as freely of the eighth century as of the fourth, it seems best to avoid it whenever possible. Instead, I shall use the terms Late Antique, Late Roman and Early Byzantine, which together, with somewhat different implications and some degree of overlap, describe the period in which the textiles were produced, and permit a better understanding of their historical background and a fuller appreciation of their artistic value.[1]

Late Antiquity is the most general term. It denotes a period extending roughly from the late third century to the middle of the seventh. This was an age of tremendous political, religious and cultural turmoil, of wars, insurrections, assassinations, riots, heresies, universal intolerance, violent sectarian strife, barbarian incursions, and the displacement of peoples on an unprecedented scale. It saw the end of the Roman Empire as we almost unfailingly conceive of it, and encompasses the transition from the ancient to the medieval world. Yet the more closely the period is studied, the more clearly one senses its continuity with the age that preceded it: political and social continuity, but cultural continuity even more, and above all, as we shall see, continuity in the realm of art.[2]

The beginning and end of Late Antiquity are marked by two supremely important political events. The first is the series of reforms instituted by the emperor Diocletian (r. A.D. 284-305) in the 280s and 290s, in the face of internal disorder and barbarian invasion. The Roman Empire was divided into eastern and western portions. The Western Empire comprised Europe from Britain and the Iberian Peninsula eastward to what is now Albania, and western North Africa to the same longitude. The Eastern Empire comprised eastern Europe, Asia Minor, Syria, Palestine and Egypt. Diocletian's reforms went much further than this, and included a restructuring of the social and economic life of the Empire along much more rigid lines.[3] The most lasting consequence of his work, however, was to insure the survival of the Roman Empire in the East, after the Western half succumbed to the Goths and other northern barbarians in the course of the fifth century. In 330 the emperor Con-

---

1. The term Early Christian is also widely used, basically as a synonym for Late Antique. This use to designate an entire period or culture can be misleading. Late Antique civilization was by no means all Christian, but the phrase Early Christian suggests it was, and denies or ignores both the quantity and the importance of the non-Christian art which the age produced.

2. Many publications are devoted to the problems of Late Antique art and civilization. Three are outstanding for their comprehensiveness and their accessibility to non-specialists. Peter Brown's *The World of Late Antiquity*, London, 1971, is a general survey of the major social and political structures and cultural trends of the period. Ernst Kitzinger's *Byzantine Art in the Making*, Cambridge, Mass., 1977, examines in detail the stylistic changes involved in the evolution from Roman to Byzantine art. *Age of Spirituality*, edited by Kurt Weitzmann, New York, 1979, is a massive exhibition catalogue arranged in such a way as to emphasize the range of subjects treated in Late Antique art and the variety of purposes for which it was created.

3. H.P. l'Orange, *Art Forms and Civic Life in the Late Roman Empire*, Princeton, 1965, is a stimulating account of the reforms of Diocletian and their implications for the study of Late Roman art.

stantine I (Emperor of the West, 313-324, sole Emperor, 324-337) established his capital at Byzantium on the Bosphorus, renaming it Constantinople. The empire of which it was the center after the fall of Rome is known as the Byzantine Empire, but its rulers and citizens considered themselves Romans. Though greatly changed with the passage of centuries, Byzantium did in fact maintain a direct line of descent from Rome until the fall of Constantinople to the Turks in 1453.

By far the most important cultural event in the Roman world during Late Antiquity is the official recognition and ultimate triumph of Christianity. Throughout the first three centuries of its history, Christianity was sometimes tacitly tolerated, sometimes violently persecuted, but never officially approved. However, in 312 or 313 Constantine established Christianity as one of the religions of the Empire, and it soon emerged as the one official religion.[4] With the exception of Julian (r. 361-363) no emperor tried to stem its growth; the Late Roman Empire was predominantly Christian, and the Byzantine Empire was for all practical purposes completely so. But despite its overwhelming importance, the Christianization of the Empire must be seen in a proper perspective. Although persecuted in its turn, paganism was not finally suppressed until the sixth century.[5] More important, the classical heritage in art and literature, inseparable from paganism, was never suppressed, but was assimilated into the developing Christian culture.

Late Antiquity ends with the spread of Islam in the seventh century. The Byzantine Empire, exhausted by a long war with Persia, was unable to resist the invading Arabs, and in the brief period between 634 and 641 lost Syria, Palestine and Egypt. These losses were permanent, imposing an eastern boundary on Christendom and marking the emergence of Islam as a great power, arguably the dominant power, in what had been the Roman world. It is at this point that the disposition of political, economic and cultural forces in the Mediterranean ceases effectively to be Roman and becomes medieval.[6]

Late Antiquity comprises both the Late Roman and the Early Byzantine periods. There is no hard-and-fast distinction between the two. Since the associations of the word Roman are largely with the west, and those of the word Byzantine are with the east, one may conveniently draw the line of demarcation at the final collapse of the Western Empire in 476. This date, however, corresponds to no radical change in the system or style of government in the East. The Byzantine monarchy, with its "Oriental" absolutism

Fig. 1. Silver plate with figure of Silenus. Byzantine, second quarter of the sixth century. Courtesy of the Dumbarton Oaks Collection, Washington, D.C.

and ceremony, is basically a continuation and elaboration of forms established in Late Roman times. The same is true in art.

Byzantine art is famous for its abstraction and otherworldliness, but especially for the early period this is a severe oversimplification. The assimilation of pagan culture by the Christian Roman Empire allowed classical themes and styles to survive virtually unchanged for centuries. This is especially true of secular art, witness a sixth-century silver dish with a figure of Silenus, the Greek god of drunkenness (fig. 1).[7] Perhaps even more striking is the extent of classical inspiration in specifically Christian works. The frescoes of New Testament scenes painted by Byzantine artists in the small church at Castelseprio near Milan (fig. 2) cannot be earlier than the seventh century and have been dated as late

---

4. A.H.M. Jones, *Constantine and the Conversion of Europe*, New York, 1948.

5. C. Mango, *Byzantium, the Empire of New Rome*, New York, 1980, pp. 89-90.

6. M. Rodinson, *Muhammed*, Harmondsworth, 1971, describes the birth of Islam, with an excellent brief summary of the political and cultural situation in the eastern Mediterranean world on the eve of the Arab invasions. For the history of the Muslim world in its early centuries see G. von Grunebaum, *Classical Islam*, Chicago, 1970.

7. Dumbarton Oaks Collection, Washington, D.C., no. 54.89.19, in E. Cruikshank Dodd, *Byzantine Silver Stamps*, Washington, 1961, no. 10, p. 73. For other, even later examples of Byzantine silver in a classical style, see *ibid.*, nos. 57, 70, 75, etc. One of the most important examples of Early Byzantine classicism is the mosaic pavement of the Imperial Palace in Constantinople; see The Walker Trust, University of St. Andrews, *The Great Palace of the Byzantine Emperors*, First Report, Oxford, 1947; Second Report, Edinburgh, 1958. The mosaic has been dated between the sixth and eighth centuries. On the problem of the date see P.J. Nordhagen, "The Mosaics of the Great Palace of the Byzantine Emperors," *Byzantinische Zeitschrift*, 56 (1963), pp. 53-68. The classical heritage is strong in Early Islamic art, which depended heavily on Byzantium for its inspiration. The most striking example is the mosaic decoration of the early eighth-century Omayyad mosque in Damascus; see K.A.C. Creswell, *Early Muslim Architecture*, 2nd ed., Oxford, 1969, vol. I, pt. 1. By far the best discussion of the problems of classical survival in Byzantine art before ca. 700 is Kitzinger, *op cit.* (note 2).

Fig. 2. Fresco of the Journey to Bethlehem. Byzantine, seventh century or later. S. Maria, Castelseprio. Author's photograph.

as the tenth.[8] Yet in their own way they are as close to the Greco-Roman tradition as the Silenus plate. There is nothing here to suggest a decisive break between Late Roman and Early Byzantine styles. These are extreme cases, however. Taken as a whole, religious art, especially, does undergo a process of rigidification and dematerialization, having as its end result the style widely recognized as Byzantine and incapable of being confused with classical or even Late Roman art. This process is neither rapid nor steady, and can for the most part be measured by degrees of departure from the classical tradition rather than sudden outright rejection of it.

The term Late Roman ceases to have value when evolution away from Roman forms and styles becomes more important than adherence to them, but there is no single way of judging when this happened. In general, from a stylistic point of view the second half of the fifth century would seem to be a turning point. For works produced after ca. 500, and in some cases after ca. 450, I prefer the term Early Byzantine, emphasizing their affinity with medieval Christian culture rather than with Antiquity.

Few Late Antique art forms are better documented than textiles in terms of sheer volume of surviving material. Tens of thousands of Late Antique textiles, all but a handful found in Egypt, are preserved in museums and private collections throughout the world. At the same time, there is no art form of the period about which we know less. What proportion of the textiles unearthed in Egypt were actually made there? Egypt was famous in antiquity as a center for textile production, and especially famous for its linen, so there is good reason to assume that many pieces, especially the linen ones, were of local manufacture.[9] Nevertheless, the largest and most important Late Roman textile in the Museum's collection (cat. no.1) bears an inscription which points to an origin in Thrace.[10] We cannot ignore the possibility that many textiles now widely identified with Egypt were imported from other parts of the Empire. The dryness of the Egyptian sand, and the custom of burying the dead fully and elaborately clothed, together created an ideal situation for the preservation of textiles.[11] This situation does not

---

8. Author's photo; see G.P. Bognetti, G. Chierici and A. de Capitani d'Arzago, *Santa Maria di Castelseprio*, Milan, 1948, and K. Weitzmann, *The Fresco Cycle of Santa Maria di Castelseprio*, Princeton, 1951.

9. For linen production in antiquity see R.J. Forbes, *Studies in Ancient Technology*, vol. 4, Leiden, 1956, pp. 27-43, especially pp. 42-43 on the importance of Egypt. However, as Forbes makes clear, the Egyptian production was nothing like a monopoly: linen of high quality was woven in a number of other parts of the ancient world.

10. H. Seyrig and L. Robert, "Sur un tissu récemment publié," *Cahiers Archéologiques*, 8 (1956), pp. 27-36.

11. M.S. Dimand, "Coptic Tunics in the Metropolitan Museum," *Metropolitan Museum Studies*, 2, pt. 2 (1930), pp. 239-252.

accurately reflect the textile production of the Late Roman Empire.

Even more vexing than the problem of origins is the problem of dating. Of all the Late Roman textiles that have been recovered, *fewer than half a dozen* of artistic importance are securely dated. This is the case despite the extensive use of grave goods in Egyptian burials, including coins, documents, and other dated or datable materials which should make it possible to fix the time of the burial with at least a fair degree of accuracy. The reason is that almost all of the textiles found in Egypt were found either by clandestine treasure-hunters or by early excavators ignorant or neglectful of archaeological methods. The contents of the graves were dispersed, often without even an inventory being kept. To know which textiles were found together would be in itself invaluable, since it would indicate which styles were roughly contemporary, but this is no longer possible. Even individual garments have regularly been cut up so that their self-contained decorations could be sold separately. As a result of such vandalism, the relative chronology of Late Roman textiles is just as tentative as the absolute chronology.

Nearly all surviving Late Roman decorated textiles are woven in the tapestry technique, either in wool and linen or entirely in wool. Some are tapestries in the popular as well as the technical sense, that is, they are independent wall-hangings with elaborate figural compositions (e.g., cat. nos. 1, 2, 20, 21). But by far the greater number of tapestries were used to decorate garments, especially tunics (e.g., cat. nos. 26 and 103). The tunics were generally woven of undyed linen; tapestry decorations could be woven into the fabric itself, or could be made separately and sewn onto the finished garment. In both cases the decoration is limited to discrete units: roundels, borders, cuffs, etc.[12] Human and animal figures, alone or in elaborate scenes, are widely used. The wearing of pictures on one's clothes is strange to our ideas of costume and fashion, but it was taken for granted in Late Antiquity. The importance of pictorial decoration largely removes Late Roman tapestry work from the realm of textile design as it is usually understood, and links it intimately with Late Roman figural art. To be appreciated fully it must not be considered in isolation, but rather as part of a broad current of style and taste that shaped the development of many art forms.[13]

The problems of appreciation which Late Antique art presents today are subtle but immense. For most modern viewers, two poles of style and expression determine the character of Western figural art. The first is classicism, understood as an awareness of the physical world, with the technical skill to capture the world in realistic or idealized form as the subject and context may demand. However much the art of our own day has departed from it, this remains the touchstone by which we judge precision of drawing or accuracy of modelling. Those very concepts have no meaning without some reference, however indirect, to the achievements of Greek and Roman art. The opposite pole is expressionism: the distortion, exaggeration, or radical simplification of forms to intensify their emotional impact. By such modifications art extends its range beyond naturalism, to encompass the extremes of human emotion or to hint at things beyond physical experience, in particular the intuition of divinity.

Almost any work of Western figural art can be seen in terms of the interaction of these tendencies, with one or the other predominating. But in Late Antique art no such principle seems to apply. I have called attention to the survival of classical styles and themes through the Early Byzantine period, yet few works preserve the classical heritage with the same purity as those I have cited. Far more often, though Late Antique art remains linked to the classical past, the connection is not a reassuring but a tantalizing or even disturbing one. Again and again the classical component seems to have become soft and imprecise, while abstraction and distortion, however pronounced, serve no recognizable expressive purpose. Every standard by which we have learned to judge a work of art seems suddenly to have lost its meaning.

Perhaps no work illustrates these unsettling qualities more clearly than the famous fourth-century silver bridal casket of Projecta, found in Rome and now in the British Museum (fig. 3).[14] The central panel of the lid depicts Venus attended by tritons and erotes, a common and easily recognizable scene from classical mythology. The style, too, is obviously of classical origin, yet on closer inspection reveals an apparent lack either of anatomical understanding or of technical command. Each of the erotes has one leg grotesquely enlarged, yet without any sense of solidity or connection with the body. The tritons' muscular arms and torsos also lack solidity, as if they were merely inflated. The central figure of Venus is boneless and weightless; likewise the erotes appear suspended in mid-air, rather than resting firmly on the tritons' backs. A morbid languor pervades the entire work.

These seeming aberrations cannot be ascribed to poor workmanship in any simple sense: the casket was made of precious material for a patron who could obviously afford the best work then available. There is a decline in skill, as measured against the best works of earlier centuries (and of later ones too: compare the Silenus plate of fig. 1), but there is also a shift in taste, a preference for softer and less substantial images. Many textiles, such as cat. no. 55, ex-

---

12. For a description of the various types of decoration, and a diagram showing their placement on the garment, see A. Baginski and A. Tidhar, *Textiles from Egypt, 4th–13th Centuries C.E.*, Jerusalem, 1980, p. 10.

13. By no means all tapestry-woven costume decorations were figural, but it is interesting to note that even abstract ornament was given a "pictorial" treatment. Complex geometric designs, which could in theory be extended to cover an entire garment, remained confined by frames in the same way as figural subjects, were used in the same places on clothes, and must therefore have been considered of equal or almost equal importance.

14. K. Shelton, *The Esquiline Treasure*, London, 1981.

Fig. 3. Silver bridal casket of Projecta. Late Roman, fourth century. Reproduced by courtesy of the Trustees of the British Museum.

hibit a similar mixture of classical inspiration and imprecise execution. Late Roman textiles have not on the whole been considered worthy of the same kind of stylistic analysis as works in other media. They appear in a very different light when it is recognized that the stylistic issues they raise are in many cases essentially the same as those raised by other arts of the period. One should not assume, however, that textiles can easily be dated by comparison with works in other media. Superficial resemblances are often deceptive, and the relation of Late Antique styles to regional origins or to particular materials and techniques is far from fully understood. The use of different art forms as evidence for dating greatly increases the chance of a misleading coincidence. This is not to say that comparisons between media are necessarily worthless, but their value depends on a meticulous regard to the history and conventions of each art form. In general, the method is perhaps best used to confirm a dating suggested by other, more concrete evidence.

So far we have been considering textiles as part of the body of Late Antique art which preserves the classical heritage, albeit with some degree of modification. But there is another tradition in the art of Late Antiquity, whose deviation from classicism goes far beyond the mere uncertainty of form that characterizes the Projecta Casket. This is most clearly illustrated by a comparison of two textiles. The first is a tapestry head in the Museum's collection, cat. no. 3.

Here, technical precision is combined with a sense of volume and a concern with shading which, if not exactly naturalistic, at least indicates an awareness of classical modes of representation. At the same time, there is a softness and indistinctness about the image, as though the face had no bone structure, no real substance. Together, these features point to a fourth-century date. In terms of technical accomplishment and classical spirit, the piece represents Late Roman figural tapestry at its ambivalent best.

It is hard to imagine a greater contrast of styles than exists between this work and a tapestry now in Brussels (fig. 4).[15] Here the classical affinity for modelling is gone: everything is abrupt and two-dimensional. The Brussels tapestry dates from the mid-fifth century, but the degree of stylization it exhibits is far in advance of the general movement away from classicism in the art of that period. In other words, there is no direct correlation between stylistic variation and the passage of time. Art flourished in many different regions and on many social levels, each of which had its own characteristics. Art which was produced at some geographic or social remove from the centers of innovation and technical refinement in the Roman world—i.e., provincial art or folk

---

15. Brussels, Musées Royaux d'Art et d'Histoire, no. 2470. For the date of the tapestry see A. Gayet, *L'Exploration des nécropoles gréco-byzantines d'Antinoë, Annales du Musée Guimet*, 30, pt. 2 (1902), Paris, p. 33.

Fig. 4. Tapestry from the grave of Aurelius Colluthus at Antinoë, Egypt (detail). Late Roman, middle of the fifth century. Reproduced by kind permission of the Musées Royaux d'Art et d'Histoire, Brussels.

art—often seems to parallel or even anticipate developments in the more cosmopolitan centers.[16] It should be kept in mind, however, that the simplifications and distortions of provincial and folk art result from diminished contact with the classical tradition, while the lessening of substance which characterizes much of Late Antique art, as represented by the Projecta Casket or the tapestry head cat. no. 3, is a sign of change and unrest within the classical tradition itself.

Perhaps the most distinctive provincial style of the Late Roman Empire is that of Egypt, known as the Coptic style (fig. 5).[17] In its most basic sense the word Coptic refers to the indigenous inhabitants of Egypt, as opposed to Romans, Arabs, or other invading peoples. Doubtless most of the art known as Coptic was indeed produced by Copts. Nevertheless the ethnic connotation of the word is confusing in discussions of art, since it implies a survival of specifically Egyptians traditions going back to the Pharaonic period. Such survivals are not common; certainly there is no fundamental continuity of style.[18] A comparison of a Pharaonic textile in the Museum's collection (fig. 6) with any textile of the Late Roman period will illustrate the stylistic difference.[19]

---

16. Kitzinger, *op. cit.* (note 2), pp. 9 ff. For a further exploration of provincial and folk styles—often called ''sub-antique'' styles—see A. Grabar, ''Le tiers monde de l'Antiquité à l'école de l'art classique et son rôle dans la formation de l'art du Moyen Age,'' *Revue de l'Art*, 18 (1972), pp. 9-26 (reprinted in Grabar, *L'Art paléochretien et l'art byzantin*, London, 1979).

17. Limestone relief of the god Dionysus. Fifth century A.D. (?) Dumbarton Oaks Collection, Washington, D.C., no. 40.60.

18. One motif which did survive into Late Antiquity is the *ankh*, the ancient Egyptian symbol of life, whose resemblance to a cross led to its absorption into the repertory of Christian art in Egypt. See H. Bober, ''On the Illumination of the Glazier Codex,'' in *Homage to a Bookman, Essays on Manuscripts, Books and Painting Written for Hans P. Kraus on his 60th Birthday*, Berlin, 1967. A stone relief in the Louvre depicts the Egyptian god Horus. This however is a thematic survival only; the style of the relief is provincial Late Roman (*Koptische Kunst: Christentum am Nil*, Essen-Bredeney, 1963, no. 77).

19. Textile Museum no. 7.3. There is also a fundamental technical difference, since in the Pharaonic piece the figures are painted on the cloth, rather than woven into it as in Late Roman work. However, it is not wholly fair to emphasize this difference: other techniques of textile decoration, including tapestry, were used by the ancient Egyptians (E. Riefstahl, *Patterned Textiles in Pharaonic Egypt*, Brooklyn, 1944). Of special interest is fig. 33 in Riefstahl's book; it shows a textile of the fourteenth century B.C. in which tapestry weaving is combined with the use of a loop pile of a kind much favored by Late Antique weavers (cf. cat. no. 84.) Again, though, there is no stylistic connection in the tapestry work.

Our most immediate association of the word Coptic is with the Coptic Church, which broke away from the Orthodox Christianity of the Eastern Empire in the fifth century and survived the Muslim conquest of Egypt two centuries later. It served then, and continues to serve, as the focus of the ethnic and cultural as well as religious identity of the Copts. The idea of a Coptic enclave that continued to produce Christian art in a Muslim-dominated society is compelling, and has tended to be projected onto the pre-Muslim period. The process is similar to that by which the conception of history embodied in the phrase Early Christian has affected our view of Late Antiquity in general.[20] Art identified as Coptic has been treated as fundamentally Christian by definition, regardless of its date. Many of the most important monuments of Coptic art, especially sculpture, have pagan mythological themes, and this has led scholars to assume that the Coptic Church maintained a unique relation to the classical tradition, using even highly erotic scenes as vehicles for Christian symbolism. There is no need for such a strained explanation: in Egypt as elsewhere, the coexistence of pagan and Christian themes is typical of Late Antique art.[21]

In speaking of Late Roman textiles I have avoided using the word Coptic. One reason is that it refers specifically to Egypt, and as I have already noted, it is by no means certain that every textile found in Egypt was made there. An equally important reason is that even if Egyptian manufacture is taken for granted in most cases, the popular associations of the word Coptic can affect the way textiles are perceived both historically and aesthetically. The concept of a Coptic Christian enclave is crucial here. It encourages one to imagine isolated groups of artisans carrying on Roman and Byzantine traditions, each generation with less understanding. This is a process of artistic debasement, and the end result must be the creation of an art in which all sense of classical form is lost. Approaching the body of Late Antique textiles from this point of view, one looks instinctively for naive art, and of course one finds it. Naive art has a near-universal appeal, while as we have seen, the more classical styles of Late Antiquity require a special effort of understanding. The incentive to make this effort can only come from an appreciation of the many sources of artistic inspiration and influence in a Late Roman provincial society. There were works of art in the classical tradition imported from the capital and elsewhere, and local imitations of them, all of various levels of quality and all subject in varying degree

Fig. 5. Limestone relief with figure of Dionysus. Late Roman (Coptic), fifth century (?). Courtesy of the Dumbarton Oaks Collection, Washington, D.C.

to the stylistic currents of the day; conservative local workshops which clung to their classical heritage even as they slipped away from it; and finally, popular traditions at many levels of relative refinement or coarseness. This vision of diversity is less easily encompassed than the simpler one of decline, but it is provocative in a way the other is not. Above all, it recognizes the importance of each of the many conventions which make up Late Roman art in Egypt.

There is a sense in which the preference for naive art is understandable. Tapestry is arguably better suited to the hard outlines and abrupt transitions typical of a popular style than to the modulations of a classicizing one. Thus by comparison to the boldness of cat. no. 7, the refinement of cat. no. 3 may seem self-conscious. There is, however, a point at which simplification ceases to be a merit. In cat. no. 24 and many works like it, style has devolved to such an extent that human and animal figures are barely recognizable. In many textile traditions, when a certain level of stylization is reached, the figures are converted into an ornamental pattern.[22] One would expect this to happen here, but as a rule it does not. Stylistically debased scenes are as much "pictures" as the finest works in the classical idiom. Indeed, it is probably a dim echo of the classical tradition, with its emphasis on the integrity of the figural image, which has

---

20. See above, note 1.
21. H. Torp, "Leda Christiana," *Institutum Romanum Norvegiae. Acta ad Archaeologiam et Artium Historiam Pertinentia*, 4 (1969), pp. 101-112. This key work views Coptic sculpture not as a separate entity but in the context of Late Roman provincial art. I am grateful to Susan MacMillan Arensberg and Gary Vikan for referring me to Torp's article. The most penetrating stylistic analysis of Coptic sculpture remains E. Kitzinger, "Notes on Early Coptic Sculpture," *Archaeologia*, 87 (1937), pp. 181-215.

22. For examples of this phenomenon see P. Johnstone, *A Guide to Greek Island Embroidery*, London, 1972, passim, and C.G. Ellis, *Early Caucasion Rugs*, Washington, D.C. (The Textile Museum), 1975, introduction and passim.

Fig. 6. Linen textile with painted figures. Egyptian, ca. 1200 B.C. The Textile Museum, Washington, D.C., no. 7.3.

petrified these scenes in their present form, rather than allowing them to be transformed into ornament. One feels that almost any degree of devolution was possible, but not that final step, the denial of the integrity and content of the image.

If it is accepted that the stylistic variation in Late Roman textiles is regional and social as well as chronological, it can no longer be assumed that the less classical a work is, the later its date must always be. The rejection of this principle makes the dating of these works seem a virtually hopeless task. However, it must be remembered that for nearly a century, scholarship in the field has been oriented toward cataloguing existing collections.[23] A collection as extensive as that of the Louvre or the Victoria and Albert Museum, or a smaller but especially fine one like that of the Textile Museum, can of course suggest the range of styles found in Late Roman textiles. What it cannot do is fully represent all those styles, their inception, maturity, and decay, their relation to one another and to the other arts of the period.

An approach is needed that is at once broader and more rigorous. On the one hand, careful comparisons with works in other media can be used to show how textiles fit into the general stylistic trends of Late Antiquity.[24] On the other hand, a new series of studies should aim at defining the characteristics of individual workshops by grouping together textiles which are identical or nearly identical in style. The catalogue entries which follow reflect this approach. In selecting examples from other collections for comparison, I have concentrated almost exclusively on stylistic relations, citing textiles which appear to be from the same workshops

---

23. There are of course exceptions, e.g., D. Shepherd, "An Icon of the Virgin: A Sixth-Century Tapestry Panel from Egypt," *Bulletin of the Cleveland Museum of Art*, 56, 3 (1969), pp. 90-120, and S.M. Arensberg, "Dionysos: A Late Antique Tapestry," *Boston Museum Bulletin*, 75 (1977), pp. 4-25. Such studies tend to concentrate on single figural textiles of the highest quality. E. Kitzinger, "The Horse and Lion Tapestry at Dumbarton Oaks," *Dumbarton Oaks Papers*, 3 (1946), pp. 1-72, also focuses on a single major textile. What makes this study unique is that the textile belongs to an essentially ornamental tradition, and that in exploring that tradition Kitzinger brings to ornament the detailed consideration usually reserved for figural art.

24. Such comparisons are attempted by P. du Bourguet, "Datation des tissus coptes en fonction des mosaiques mediterranéennes, *Ars Orientalis*, 3 (1959), pp. 189-192. Unfortunately his choice of comparative material is not systematic, nor do the comparisons themselves rest on a unified concept of style. As a result they cannot serve as the basis for a reliable dating system.

Fig. 7. Tapestry square with animal, floral and interlace motifs. Late Roman, fifth century. The Metropolitan Museum of Art, New York, no. 89.18.223, purchase.

as the pieces under discussion, or which resemble them closely enough to help define a period style.[25] Once workshop groups have been established, the next step is to analyze the variations within them, to determine which changes reflect the passage of time, and which ones reflect the influence of other weaving traditions. Textiles in which features typical of two or more groups appear side by side are especially important, since they indicate which workshops were active at the same time. An example is fig. 7, a tapestry in the Metropolitan Museum of Art in New York, which combines interlace motifs with the historically separate theme of animals enclosed by highly stylized plant forms.[26] By these means it is possible to construct a relative chronology for Late Roman textiles. The final step is that of translating the relative chronology into an absolute one by establishing the relation of the various workshop groups to the small number of textiles whose dating is not in question. Needless to say, such an investigation will be of value only if it takes account of a far greater number of textiles than can be found in any one collection.

I have tried to illustrate this approach by applying it to a particular group of textiles, those with interlace patterns see Appendix I. Even within the limits of this group, I have been obliged to confine myself to works in the Textile Museum's collection, introducing others only as necessary to give a coherent picture of the way the patterns evolved. More extensive exploration is beyond the scope of this catalogue. To correlate stylistic developments in the entire corpus of Late Antique textiles, numbering in the tens of thousands, is probably beyond the scope of any single study. It is, however, well within the scope of cooperative effort by the next generation of scholars in textile history and Late Antique art. The majority of pieces in this catalogue are presented in the hope that they will serve as raw material for future studies. The value of such a shared endeavor would be immense. Not only would it restore an important and fascinating body of work to its proper place in the estimation of scholars and laymen, it would shed new light on the processes of influence and of the growth and decay of styles in Late Antiquity.

---

25. P. du Bourguet, *Musée national du Louvre. Catalogue des étoffes coptes*, Paris, 1964, is the only catalogue of Late Antique textiles in which an awareness of workshop groups has significantly affected the arrangement of material.

26. Unpublished. Metropolitan Museum, no. 89.18.223.

Plate 1, cat. no. 1

Plate 2, cat. no. 2

Plate 3, cat. no. 3

Plate 4, cat. no. 7

Plate 5, cat. no. 9

Plate 6, cat. no. 11

Plate 7, cat. no. 83

Plate 8, cat. no. 108

TAPESTRIES

Almost all the patterned textiles which survive from Late Roman times are tapestries. The tapestry loom is a simple device of great antiquity, essentially a vertical frame designed to hold the warp in place evenly and tightly.[1] The weaver builds up the pattern with discontinuous wefts of one or more colors.[2] Color and pattern can be changed at will; the only limitations on what can be represented are those imposed by the coarseness or fineness of the warp and weft, and by the weaver's patience. In this respect tapestry weaving has little in common with weaving on more complex looms, which require that the pattern be programmed before weaving begins.[3] This is not to say that Late Roman tapestry is an art of improvisation: its best patterns are carefully thought out and meticulously executed. Still, many examples have a directness and spontaneity which cannot be unrelated to the comparative freedom of the technique.

The fibers used in almost all Late Roman tapestry weaving are wool and linen.[4] The tapestries themselves fall into two main categories, polychrome and monochrome (cat. nos. 1–24 and 25–103, respectively). By far the most frequently used color in monochrome tapestries is purple, though other colors, notably red and blue, were also used.[5] Literally speaking, there is no hard-and-fast distinction between the two types: monochrome pieces often make considerable use of highlights in other colors. In practice, polychrome tapestries can be said to be those which use a full range of colors, for the sake either of naturalism (cat. no. 9) or of decorative exuberance (cat. no. 11). Late Roman tapestries were created for a variety of purposes, from delicate garment trimmings to large curtains and wall hangings. In general, neither type of tapestry was restricted to a specific function or functions, though there are exceptions to this principle. No monochrome hangings survive which approach the size of cat. no. 1. The largest seem to be the group to which cat. no. 42 belongs, and it is unlikely that much bigger ones were woven. Devices which successfully convey a sense of detail and three-dimensionality in a tiny work like cat. no. 25 rely on delicacy for their effect. They would be ridiculous on a large scale. The central figure of cat. no. 42 is dramatic because of its contrast with the light ground, but the effect would be dull and oppressive if the figure were much larger.

There are patterns, too, which were rarely if ever attempted in polychrome. Cat. no. 16 is probably as close as any polychrome piece to the intricate geometric and interlace compositions which were one of the great achievements of the monochrome tradition. Evidently it was felt that the precision of drawing on which such designs depended would be eclipsed by multiple or brilliant colors.

The use of a single color rules out, by definition, the possibility of a fully naturalistic style, in the sense of a style

---

1. A. Geijer: *A History of Textile Art*, London, 1979, pp. 23-24.
2. For a detailed description of tapestry weaves see I. Emery: *The Primary Structures of Fabrics*, Washington, D.C. (The Textile Museum), 1966 (2nd ed. 1980), pp. 78-84.
3. See below, pp. 96 ff.
4. A few Late Roman silk tapestries survive. See for example A. Geijer, "The Viminacium Gold Tapestry," *Meddelanden fran Lunds Universitets Historiska Museum*, 1964-65, pp. 223-236, and D. Renner, "Spätantike figurliche Purpurwirkereien," in M. Flury-Lemberg and K. Stollers, ed.: *Documenta Textilia, Festschrift für Sigrid Müller-Christensen*, Munich, 1981, pp. 82-94, figs. 1 and 2.
5. Tyrian or "true" purple, made from the *murex* shellfish, was the most highly valued of all dyes. Except for the very finest grades it does not seem, as many people believe, to have been restricted to Imperial use. What was prohibited was apparently the wearing of anything that could be mistaken for a *completely* purple garment, since this was an Imperial prerogative (M. Reinhold: *History of Purple as a Status Symbol in Antiquity*, Brussels, 1970). Nevertheless true purple was prohibitively expensive for most people, and imitations were in wide use. Chemical tests are required to determine the composition of dyes, but it is likely that most of the "purple" textiles now preserved, including those illustrated here, were dyed with a combination of madder and indigo.

which attempts to capture the colors as well as the forms of the physical world. (The touches of color which frequently brighten monochrome work are a decorative adjunct and have nothing to do with naturalism.) Working within this convention the weaver has two options. The first is to attempt to triumph over its built-in limitations by creating the most lifelike possible effect by means of line alone (cat. nos. 25 and 27B). This is the principle of drawing as opposed to painting. The second option is to convert the technical limitation into an advantage. By largely or completely ignoring shading and detail, and concentrating on silhouette, the artist could achieve an effect which has no real parallel in drawing. Without individuating or even anatomical detail, the figures convey an immediate overall impression rather than encouraging closer scrutiny. Occasionally the effects achieved in this manner approach the graceful stylization of true ornament (cat. no. 35). More often the effect is not so much graceful as bold, casual, and suggestive of movement (cat. nos. 44, 45 and the side panels in 42). While it may not appeal to every modern viewer, the silhouette style should be recognized as one of the most important contributions of Late Roman tapestry weavers. It is especially interesting as an example of the influence of technique on style.

Polychrome tapestry is subject to a completely different set of technical limitations. It is comparable to painting in that it has the means to encompass the colors as well as the forms of the natural world. However, unlike painting, it is for all practical purposes incapable of true modulation of color. Comparable effects are achieved by dovetailing one color into another.[6] Like the monochrome convention, this technical dictate offers the weaver two alternatives. The first is to make the dovetailing as fine as possible, so that the colors will effectively blend, producing a painterly effect when viewed from the proper distance. Cat. nos. 1 and 3 are examples of the painterly approach to tapestry. The danger of this approach is that the transitions between colors are almost never perfectly fluid. The result is a certain awkwardness or self-consciousness vis-à-vis painting, noticeable precisely because the effect so closely approaches the other medium and invites comparison with it. The other alternative is to avoid the problem altogether by not trying to emulate painting, relying instead on large areas of bold, unmodulated color, highly conventionalized detail, or both. Cat. nos. 7 and 11 exemplify this approach, which in skilled hands produces folk art of the very highest quality.

It thus appears that monochrome and polychrome tapestry each comprise two modes. One seeks through virtuosity to overcome the limitations of technique, by imitating drawing or painting. The other utilizes and emphasizes those limitations to create a simpler, more decorative effect.[7] Although the tapestries illustrated here encompass a broad spectrum of styles, these fundamental categories may give the modern viewer a better understanding of the goals and achievements of Late Roman weaving.

On a different note it should be mentioned that the resemblance of polychrome tapestry to painting—and mosaic—makes it a less isolated art from than monochrome, in two senses. It is more immediately accessible to the layman, and it is the province of less specialized study. Works like cat. nos. 1, 3 and 9 belong to the mainstream of Late Roman representational art in a way that few works in monochrome can be said to do. This would seem to suggest that they can be studied more safely than the monochromes in relation to works in other media, and are therefore easier to date and localize. In fact, however, the opposite may be true. The paintings and mosaics which provide points of comparison are often themselves the subject of controversy. Themes and styles could persist for generations; the changes they underwent are often subtle and far from fully understood. The correspondences between tapestry and other arts are often close, but because of the differences inherent in the media they can never be exact. Even if a tapestry were intended as an accurate copy of a painting or mosaic, a quirk of individual or workshop style could make it resemble, to modern eyes, a work of a very different time or place. Finally, far fewer tapestries of high quality survive in polychrome than in monochrome, making it difficult if not impossible to trace the development of individual workshops or to formulate the characteristics of a period style.

---

6. The word "dovetailing" in this context is not a structural term, but refers only to the way colors appear to the eye. On the structural meaning of dovetailing in tapestry weaving, see Emery, *op. cit.* (note 2), p. 80. In the technical descriptions of individual tapestries the word is used in its structural sense only.

---

7. Cat. no. 21 seems to be an attempt to combine the two approaches. The result is not without charm, but is hardly a successful synthesis

(Color Plate 1)

1 Curtain or hanging with erotes, animals, and floral and geometric motifs.
Fourth century

This is the largest and arguably the most important Late Roman tapestry yet discovered. It makes use of a number of unrelated motifs to create a purely decorative composition. The figure style of the tapestry, its general artistic background and its date, are discussed by S.M. Arensberg ("Dionysos," passim). A pair of tapestry squares with erotes, in the Pushkin Museum, are also close in style (Shurinova; *Coptic Textiles*, nos. 16 and 17). The same museum furnishes extremely close parallels to the style of the interlace bands in the second registers from top and bottom (Shurinova, nos. 40 and 41). This interlace represents the same approximate stage of evolution as cat. no. 84 and fig. 4 of Appendix I. For an analogy to the interlace in the top and bottom registers of the curtain, cf. Kendrick: *Catalogue of Textiles*, vol. I, no. 229, pl. 32.

Another large tapestry in the Textile Museum, cat. no. 2, is almost certainly a product of the same workshop as no. 1: note the style of the birds as well as the identical squares containing rosettes (Wace, "Preliminary Historical Study"). The place of origin of no. 1, and thus presumably of no. 2 as well, is the subject of controversy. The eros at the top left holds a garland enclosing an inscription. H. Seyrig and L. Robert have reconstructed it to read *Herakleias*—"at Herakleia"—and argued that it refers to Herakleia Perinthos, now Ereğli, on the Sea of Marmora near Constantinople, which was a weaving center in Late Antiquity ("Sur un tissu récemment publié"). However their reading of the inscription has been questioned, as has their identification of the site: there were many towns called Herakleia, and others beside this one may have supported tapestry workshops.

Tapestry over one warp, slit and dovetailed; weft wrapping; eccentric wefts
Warp: undyed wool
Weft: undyed linen, nineteen colors of wool (see Appendix II)
10'8" x 5'11" (3.25 m. x 1.8 m.)
Acquired in 1950 from Phocion Tano, Cairo
Published: A.J.B. Wace, "Preliminary Historical Study: A Late Roman Tapestry from Egypt," *Textile Museum Workshop Notes*, Paper no. 9, 1954; F.S. Greene, "The Cleaning and Mounting of a Large Wool Tapestry," *Studies in Conservation*, II, 1 (1955) pp. 1-16; H. Seyrig and L. Robert, "Sur un tissu récemment publié," *Cahiers Archéologiques*, 9 (1956), pp. 27-36; J. Beckwith, "Coptic Textiles," *CIBA Review*, vol. 12, no. 133 (1959), p. 4 (mention only); O.L. Varela, "Photographing Textiles for a Museum," *Textile Museum Journal*, 1 (1962), pp. 23-29, figs. 9 and 10; M.-Th. Picard-Schmitter, "Une tapisserie hellénistique d'Antinoë, au Musée du Louvre," *Monuments Piot*, 52 (1962) p. 48, fig. 13; L. Mackie and A.P. Rowe: *Master-*

No. 1 (detail)

pieces in the Textile Museum, Washington (Textile Museum), 1976, fig. 1; S.M. Arensberg, "Dionysos: A Late Roman Tapestry," *Boston Museum Bulletin*, 75 (1977), pp. 4-25

71.118

(Color plate 2)

2 Curtain or hanging with an architectural frame
Fourth Century

Two large columns support a gable. The enclosed space is filled with an elegant grid pattern of highly stylized vine leaves; the grid in turn contains birds and bunches of grapes. It is possible that the composition as a whole is intended to represent, or at least suggest, a curtain hung between two columns—a playful reflection of the way the tapestry was actually meant to be used.

A.J.B. Wace has pointed to the use, in both this tapestry and cat. no. 1, of large square frames with dotted sides, enclosing rosettes (Wace, "Preliminary Historical Study.") He suggests on this basis that the two works came from the same workshop. The similarity in the depiction of birds in the two tapestries makes this conclusion a virtual certainty. For the question of the workshop's location, see cat. no. 1.

Tapestry over one warp, slit and dovetailed; weft wrapping; eccentric wefts
Warp: undyed wool
Weft: red, tan, blue, orange, several shades of green, and undyed wool; undyed linen
85" x 46" (213.4 cm x 117 cm)
Acquired in 1925 from Joseph Brummer, New York
Exhibited: "Found in Egypt," Textile Museum, 1963; "Masterpieces in the Textile Museum," Textile Museum, 1975
Published: A.J.B. Wace, "Preliminary Historical Study: A Late Roman Tapestry from Egypt," *Textile Museum Workshop Notes*, Paper no. 9, 1954, pl. 2

71.18

(Color plate 3)

3 Head of a mythological figure (a Season?)
Fourth century

The figure is difficult to identify with certainty. Even the gender is indistinct, though it is probably male. The right hand holds what seems to be a *thyrsus*, an attribute of Dionysus and his followers; the right hand holds an unidentified object which may be a sheaf of grain or a basket of fruit. The closest parallel for the attributes and the androgynous face is probably to be found in the male figures representing the Seasons who accompany Dionysus on a third-century sarcophagus in the Metropolitan Museum of Art (F. Matz: *Die dionysischen Sarkophage*, vol. 4, Berlin, 1977, no. 258). The objects they hold are clearly baskets, though of unusual shape.

Tapestry over one warp, slit and dovetailed; eccentric wefts
Warp: undyed wool
Weft: wool in three shades each of pink, blue and green, plus tan, orange, brown, yellow and undyed
14¼" x 11⅛" (36.3 cm x 28.4 cm)
Acquired in 1927 from Paul Mallon, Paris
Exhibited: "Festival of Religious Arts," First Baptist Church, Washington, 1962
Published: D. Shepherd, "An Icon of the Virgin," *Bulletin of the Cleveland Museum of Art*, 56 (1969), p. 110, fig. 20

71.10

4 Square ornament with a bust of Dionysus
Fifth century

This tapestry is identical in style to examples in the Louvre and the Brooklyn Musuem. See du Bourguet: *Catalogue des étoffes coptes*, nos. B20 and B21, and Thompson: *Coptic Textiles in the Brooklyn Museum*, no. 9.

Tapestry over one warp, slit and dovetailed; weft wrapping; eccentric wefts
Warp: undyed linen
Weft: undyed, purple, gold, greenish-blue, pink, red, tan, light green and black wool.
10⅝" x 10¼" (27 cm x 26 cm)
Acquired in 1954 from Phocion Tano, Cairo
Exhibited: "Found in Egypt," Textile Museum, 1963
71.132

5 Fragment representing a city-goddess (tuchē)
Sixth century (?)

The subject is the *tuchē* or tutelary goddess of Alexandria, identifiable by her attributes, the ibis and cornucopia. The mural crown which she wears betokens an urban as opposed to a rural community. The halo is of pre-Christian origin, and as used here has nothing to do with Christianity. (This information is taken from a note by Henri Seyrig, written on the back of a photograph of the tapestry and dated 1944.)

Tapestry over plied warps, slit and dovetailed; weft wrapping; eccentric wefts
Warp: undyed linen
Weft: undyed linen; red, pink, yellow, blue-green, yellow-green, three shades of blue, light and dark brown wool
4¾" x 4½" (12 cm x 11.5 cm)
Acquired in 1942 from Phocion Tano, Cairo
Exhibited: Hartford, Wadsworth Atheneum, and Baltimore, Museum of Art, 1951-52
Published: A.C. Weibel: *Two Thousand Years of Tapestry Weaving*, Hartford, 1951
71.80

6 Tunic decoration (?) with a bust of a woman

Fifth century

The border recalls patterns associated with, and in some cases derived from, the kind of interlace that was popular around the middle of the fifth century (cf. cat. no. 87). More importantly, the geometric simplification of the bust is comparable to that of a tapestry in Brussels, datable shortly after 450 (Introduction, fig. 4). A tapestry in the Pushkin Museum, though not closely related, combines a crude figure style with fifth century interlace, reinforcing the conclusion that folk styles occur at a relatively early date (Shurinova: *Coptic Textiles*, no. 85).

Tapestry over paired warps, slit and dovetailed; weft wrapping; eccentric wefts
Warp: undyed linen
Weft: (tapestry) undyed linen, blue, black, red, orange, yellow, blue-green, pink, purple and undyed wool; (plain weave) undyed linen
6¼" x 5⅞" (15.9 cm x 14.9 cm) (tapestry only)
Acquired in 1952 from Phocion Tano, Cairo
711.40

(Color plate 4)

7 Rectangular panel with a bust of a woman

Fifth century or later

For the very highly stylized vine motif cf. du Bourguet: *Catalogue des étoffes coptes*, nos. D150 and D151, and Wulff and Volbach: *Spätantike und koptische Stoffe*, nos. 11442 and 11443, pl. 79. This tapestry may also be related to Wulff and Volbach, no. 4652, pl. 21, which shares its bold, simple forms and rather somber color scheme (note especially the use of a dark brick red). The comparison is of special interest because the tapestry illustrated by Wulff and Volbach includes human figures in monochrome silhouette, executed with great freedom and fluidity. If the two tapestries are related, then the stiffness of the image in the Textile Museum's example must be regarded as a deliberately chosen decorative mode, rather than as a sign of late date or of isolation from the sources of classical inspiration.

Tapestry over paired warps, slit and dovetailed; weft wrapping; eccentric wefts
Warp: undyed linen
Weft: undyed linen; undyed, light and dark blue, green, red and ochre wool
12⅜" x 9⅞" (31.5 cm x 24.9 cm)
Acquired in 1948 from Phocion Tano, Cairo
72.121

8 Fragment of tunic decoration with an eros surrounded by hares
Fifth century

A pair of roundels in the Louvre are executed in a similar style (du Bourguet: *Catalogue des étoffes coptes*, nos. D36 and D37).

Slit tapestry over paired warps; weft wrapping; eccentric wefts
Warp: undyed linen
Weft: undyed linen; red, green, blue, ochre and brown wool
Maximum dimension: 5⅜" (13.7 cm)
Acquired in 1948 from Phocion Tano, Cairo
72.128

(Color plate 5)

9 Fragment with the forequarters of a hare
Fourth century or later

Tapestry over one warp, slit and dovetailed; weft wrapping; eccentric wefts
Warp: undyed wool
Weft: undyed, blue, navy, yellow, green, pink and red wool
5¼" x 4⅝" (13.1 cm x 11.8 cm)
Acquired in 1948 from Michel Abemayor, New York
72.165

10 Ornament from a curtain (?) depicting a deer
Fifth or sixth century

For an example of a curtain with leaf-shaped tapestry ornaments, see du Bourguet: *Catalogue des étoffes coptes*, no. E91. Curtains of a similar type are discussed by V. Gervers, "An Early Christian Curtain in the Royal Ontario Museum," in Gervers, ed.: *Studies in Textile History*, Toronto, 1977, pp. 56-81.

Tapestry over plied warps, slit and dovetailed; eccentric wefts
Warp: undyed linen
Weft: undyed linen; dark and light green, blue, yellow, dark brown, aqua, pink and rose wool
7" x 6¾" (18 cm x 17 cm)
Acquired in 1937 from Phocion Tano, Cairo
Exhibited: Brooklyn Museum, 1941; Rhode Island School of Design Museum, 1947; Andover, Addison Gallery (Phillips Academy), 1947; Hartford, Wadsworth Atheneum, and Baltimore, Museum of Art, 1951-52
Published: *Pagan and Christian Egypt*, Brooklyn, 1941, no. 256; A.C. Weibel: *Two Thousand Years of Tapestry Weaving*, Hartford, 1951, cat. no. 20.
71.63

(Color plate 6)

11 Fragment of a curtain or hanging with a panther

Sixth century or later

Tapestry over one warp, slit and dovetailed; weft wrapping; eccentric wefts; plain weave ground
Warp: undyed wool
Weft: (tapestry) undyed linen; undyed, red, blue, green, pink, and ochre wool; (plain weave) undyed wool
22½" x 12½" (72.5 cm x 31.8 cm)
Acquired in 1944 from Robert McClenahan, Philadelphia
72.103

12 Fragment of a rinceau

Late fourth or early fifth century

A pair of tapestry squares in the Kunsthistorisches Museum, Vienna, provides the closest parallel to this fragment (K. Wessel: *Coptic Art in Early Christian Egypt*, New York, 1965, figs. 112 and 113, p. 188). See also Zaloscer: *Ägyptische Wirkereien*, pl. 4; Shurinova: *Coptic Textiles*, no. 153; Kendrick: *Catalogue of Textiles*, vol. I, no. 176, pl. 24.

Tapestry over one warp, slit and dovetailed; eccentric wefts
Warp: red wool
Weft: undyed, purple, pink, rust, yellow, dark green, light and dark blue wool
7¼" x 5⅞" (18.2 cm x 15 cm)
Acquired in 1927 from the Anderson Galleries, New York (from the sale of the Kevorkian collection)
71.5

13 Fragment of a curtain or hanging with floral patterns

Fifth century(?)

This fragment almost certainly formed part of a large hanging of the type represented by cat. no. 42. It is identical in style to a tapestry fragment in the Kunstgewerbemuseum, Zurich, inv. no. 11179 (E. Billeter: *Aussereuropäische Textilien,* p. 39). Cf. also Wulff and Volbach: *Spätantike and koptische Stoffe,* nos. 9078, pl. 7; 9230, pl. 44; and 9232, pl. 45.

Tapestry over paired, triple or quadruple warps, slit and dovetailed; eccentric wefts
Warp: undyed linen
Weft: undyed linen; red, pink, maroon, three shades of green, yellow and orange wool
30¾" x 10⅞" (78 cm x 27.5 cm)
Acquired in 1932 from Herbert Weissberger, New York
Exhibited: "Found in Egypt," Textile Museum, 1963
71.47

14 Cushion cover (?) with a basket of flowers

Fifth century

Tapestry over paired warps, slit and dovetailed; weft wrapping; eccentric wefts; plain weave ground with supplementary wefts and weft loops at regular intervals

Warp: undyed linen

Weft: (tapestry) undyed linen, red, pink, coral, green, blue, yellow and rust wool; (plain weave and loops) undyed linen

22¾" x 20" (58 cm x 51 cm) (total, including fringe)
11⅞" x 10⅝" (30.2 cm x 27 cm) (tapestry only)
Acquired in 1941 from Phocion Tano, Cairo
Exhibited: "A Textile Museum Sampler," Textile Museum, 1967-68
71.78

15 Decoration from a curtain (?) with addorsed parakeets
Sixth century

A curtain in the Louvre is decorated with a number of small tapestry panels depicting parrots or parakeets. It therefore not only offers a thematic and stylistic parallel, but also suggests how the Textile Museum's example may have been used (du Bourguet: *Catalogue des étoffes coptes*, no. E116). For other curtains with similar decorative schemes cf. V. Gervers, "An Early Christian Curtain in the Royal Ontario Museum" in Gervers, ed., *Studies in Textile History*, Toronto, 1977, pp. 56-81.

Slit tapestry over one warp; weft wrapping; eccentric wefts
Warp: undyed linen
Weft: undyed linen; undyed, brown, orange, light and dark green, and dark blue wool
4⅞" x 3¾" (12.5 cm x 9.5 cm)
Acquired in 1951 from Phocion Tano, Cairo
11.27

16 Tunic decoration (?) with interlace and crosses
Fifth or sixth century

Tapestry over one warp, slit and dovetailed; weft wrapping; eccentric wefts
Warp: orange wool
Weft: blue, green, red, white, and yellow-orange wool
7¼" x 6¾" (18 cm x 17 cm)
Acquired in 1927 from the Anderson Galleries, New York (from the sale of the Kevorkian collection)
Published: Anderson Galleries: *The H. Kevorkian Collection of Near and Far Eastern Art*, cat. no. 43
71.4

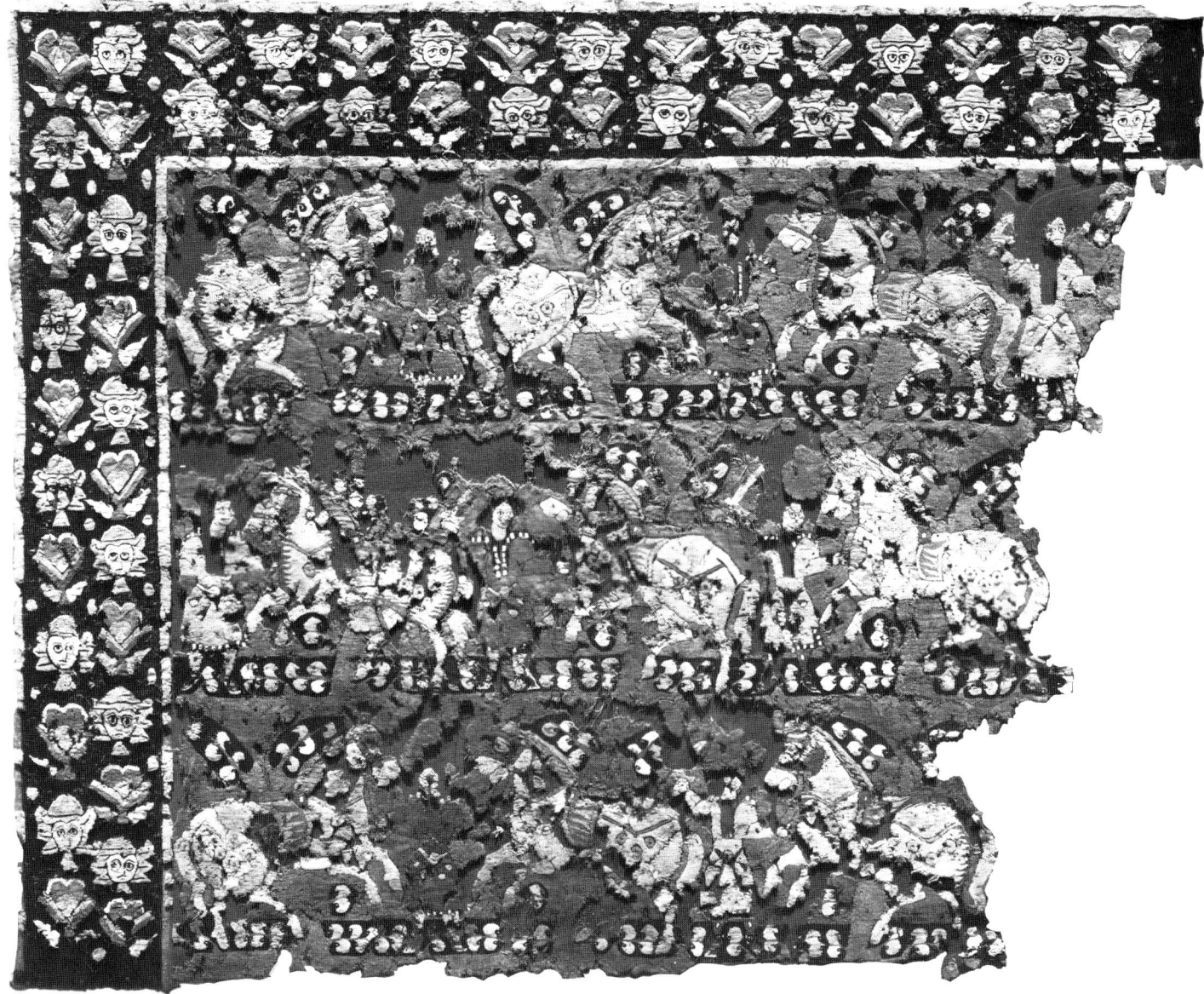

17 Hanging with horses and warriors
Sixth century

Nine horses, each held by a standing figure, stand in front of highly stylized trees. Some of the figures hold a horse's bridle in each hand, others hold a bridle in one hand and a sword in the other. The border consists of alternating heads and heart-shaped palmettes. This tapestry is one of a group which attest to a fascination with Persian motifs in the Eastern Mediterranean world during the sixth century. The costume of the warriors, the stepped patches of color on the horses, the circular trappings called phalerae suspended from bands encircling each horse horizontally, and the motifs in the border, all have Persian associations. On this current of taste see Kitzinger, "The Horse and Lion Tapestry."

A closely similar border is used in cat. no. 18. For other examples of the use of detached heads as a decorative motif, cf. tapestries in the Nelson Gallery, Kansas City (Kitzinger, op. cit., fig. 47); in the Museum of Fine Arts, Boston (Weibel: *Two Thousand Years of Textiles*, cat. no. 33); and in the Musée Historique des Tissus, Lyon (G. de Francovich, "L'Egitto, la Siria, Costantinopoli: problemi di metodo," *Rivista dell'Istituto Nazionale d'Archeologia e Storia dell'Arte*, nos. 11-12 (1963), pp. 83-229, esp. fig. 141, p. 190). For the stepped patterns on the horses cf. a tapestry in the Yale University Art Museum (Weibel, op. cit., cat. no. 30). The phalera is described in A. Alföldi and E. Cruikshank, "A Sassanian Silver Phalera at Dumbarton Oaks," *Dumbarton Oaks Papers*, 11 (1957), pp. 237-245. For Persian costumes see E.H. Peck, "The Representation of Costumes in the Reliefs of Taq-i Bustan," *Artibus Asiae*, 31 (1969), pp. 101-146.

Tapestry over one warp, slit and dovetailed; eccentric wefts
Warp: red wool
Weft: red, light and dark blue, light and dark green, white, pink, yellow and coral wool
46" x 38½" (117 cm x 97 cm)
Acquired in 1928 from Hagop Kevorkian, New York
Exhibited: Brooklyn Museum, 1941; "Found in Egypt," Textile Museum, 1963
Published: *Pagan and Christian Egypt*, Brooklyn, 1941, cat. no. 242, illus; Kitzinger, "The Horse and Lion Tapestry," fig. 46; O.L. Varela, "Photographing Textiles for a Museum," *Textile Museum Journal*, I:1 (1962), p. 29, figs. 11 and 12.
71.14

18 Hanging with a grid pattern
Sixth century

The border of heads and palmettes in this tapestry is similar to that of cat. no. 17. The closest parallel for the pattern as a whole is a tapestry at Dumbarton Oaks (Weibel: *Two Thousand Years of Textiles*, no. 5). For other grid patterns cf. cat. nos. 112-114. The Persian associations of this pattern are discussed by Kitzinger in "The Horse and Lion Tapestry." For an example of a very similar grid depicted in a Persian monument see E.H. Peck, "The Representation of Costumes in the Reliefs of Taq-i Bustan," *Artibus Asiae*, 31 (1969), pp. 101-146, pl. 16.

Slit tapestry over one warp; eccentric wefts
Warp: undyed wool
Weft: undyed, light and dark blue, green, red and ochre wool
47½" x 29¼" (120.8 cm x 71.5 cm)
Acquired in 1931 from Arthur Upham Pope, New York
Exhibited: Brooklyn Museum, 1941; "Found in Egypt," Textile Museum, 1953
Published: *The American Magazine of Art*, 22 (1931), pl. facing p. 335; Kitzinger, "The Horse and Lion Tapestry," p. 44ff. and fig. 45; *Pagan and Christian Egypt*, Brooklyn, 1941, cat. no. 239; D.N. Wilber, "'Pagan and Christian Egypt,' an Exhibition," *Ars Islamica*, 9 (1942), p. 153, fig. 1
71.33

19 Hanging with pairs of panthers and horses in roundels

Sixth century

This tapestry is of the same general type as cat. no. 17, insofar as it reflects Persian influence. In particular, Kitzinger compares the depiction of the panthers to those in the border of the Dumbarton Oaks Horse and Lion Tapestry, which he argues are strongly Persian in style ("The Horse and Lion Tapestry," p. 40). However, the theme of symmetrically paired animals in repeated roundels is probably of Byzantine origin (J. Trilling: *The Medallion Style in Late Roman and Early Byzantine Mosaics and Textiles to c. A.D. 600*, Harvard University doctoral dissertation, 1980).

The inscription to the left of the top central roundel reads *philopokia*—"love of wool." Kitzinger raises the possibility that this is a kind of trademark, but notes that the inscription is written in ink rather than woven into the tapestry, and may therefore have been added later (Kitzinger, *op. cit.*, n. 173).

Slit tapestry over one warp; eccentric wefts
Warp: blue wool
Weft: undyed linen; red, dark blue, green and tan wool
60" x 42½" (152 cm x 107.4 cm)
Acquired in 1932 from Khawam Brothers, Cairo
Exhibited: Brooklyn Museum, 1941; Hartford, Wadsworth Atheneum, and Baltimore, Museum of Art, 1951-52; "Found in Egypt," Textile Museum, 1963
Published: *Pagan and Christian Egypt*, Brooklyn, 1941, cat. no. 241, illus.; Kitzinger, "The Horse and Lion Tapestry," pp. 41ff; Weibel: *Two Thousand Years of Tapestry Weaving*, Hartford, 1951, no. 38; D. Thompson, "Observations on Some Monumental Egyptian Tapestries," *Irene Emery Roundtable on Museum Textiles, 1974 Proceedings*, Washington (Textile Museum), 1975, p. 10 (abstract only)

71.51

20 Hanging with nereids and dolphins in a Nilotic setting
Sixth century

On a field consisting mainly of highly stylized papyrus plants, male figures hold ibis, birds identified with Egypt. At the corners of the field four nereids, drawn on a larger scale, hang seemingly suspended in front of dolphins. They hold scarves which billow over their heads. A fifth nereid is at the center of the field; this area is too badly damaged for her posture or activity to be reconstructed with certainty. The border consists of winged horses separated by trees.

A tapestry in the Abegg-Stiftung Bern in Riggisberg depicts a nereid in a similar attitude, although she holds a wine flask rather than a scarf (M. Lemberg and B. Schmedding, *Abegg-Stiftung Bern in Riggisberg*, II, *Textilien,* Schweizer Heimatbücher, 17 (3-4), Bern, 1973, pl. 3). In general, however, the design of the central field is much more closely related to floor mosaics than to other surviving textiles. It combines elements from two distinct traditions, the Nile scene and the representation of marine divinities. For examples of the former see L. Foucher, "Les mosaiques nilotiques africaines," *La mosaique gréco-romaine*, Paris (Centre national de la recherche scientifique), 1965, pp. 137-143. For the latter see J. Lassus, "Vénus marine," *La mosaique*, pp. 175-189; also I. Lavin, "The Hunting Mosaics of Antioch and their Sources," *Dumbarton Oaks Papers*, 17 (1963), pp. 181-286, figs. 36, 43, 62, 71, etc. Note that in several cases (including the Bern tapestry) the nereids are depicted, as here, suspended in front of the dolphins rather than astride them. A limestone relief in Trieste also represents nereids in similar attitudes and with a comparable degree of stylization (*Age of Spirituality*, no. 151, p. 172).

Slit tapestry over one warp; weft wrapping; eccentric wefts
Warp: red wool, blue wool
Weft: undyed linen; undyed, red, pink, light and dark blue, light and dark green wool
90½" x 61½" (212 cm x 162 cm)
Acquired in 1950 from Phocion Tano, Cairo
Exhibited: "Found in Egypt," Textile Museum, 1963; "Masterpieces in the Textile Museum," Textile Museum, 1976; Metropolitan Museum of Art, 1977
Published: D. Thompson, "Observations on Some Monumental Egyptian Tapestries," *Irene Emery Roundtable on Museum Textiles, 1974 Proceedings*, Washington (Textile Museum), 1975, p. 10 (abstract only); *Age of Spirituality*, New York, 1977, no. 150, pp. 171-172 and color plate IV
1.48

21 Fragment of a hanging with a hunting scene

Sixth century

This tapestry, a fragment of a larger scene, has been said to represent Meleager and Atalanta at the Calydonian boar hunt. However, there is no evidence to support this conclusion. The animal at the top center, above the mounted Amazon, is a lion. Other, much more fragmentary animals are also visible, but there is no indication that the scene ever included a boar.

Slit tapestry over one warp; weft wrapping; eccentric wefts
Warp: undyed wool
Weft: undyed, red, pink, three shades of green, three shades of blue, brown, beige, tan, yellow and rust wool
41¾" x 31½" (106 cm x 80 cm)
Acquired in 1946 from Paul Mallon, Paris
Exhibited: American Federation of Arts Loan Exhibition, "Abstract Art in Ancient Textiles," 1959-60; "Found in Egypt," Textile Museum, 1963; "Wissa Wassef Tapestries from Egypt," Textile Museum, 1975; Metropolitan Museum of Art, 1977
Published: O.L. Varela, "Photographing Textiles for a Museum," *Textile Museum Journal* 1 (1962), figs. 7 and 8; D. Thompson, "Observations on Some Monumental Egyptian Tapestries," *Irene Emery Roundtable on Museum Textiles, 1974 Proceedings*, Washington (Textile Museum), 1975, p. 210 (abstract only); *Age of Spirituality*, New York, 1977, no. 142, p. 164
71.90

22 Fragment depicting a horse

Sixth Century

The ribbons on the legs and tail of the horse are a Persian motif, and are meant to confer special importance on the animal. For other examples see Guimet: *Les portraits d'Antinoë*, pl. 5a (facing p.8) and Volbach: *Early Decorative Textiles*, pl. 60.

Slit tapestry over one warp; weft wrapping; eccentric wefts
Warp: red wool
Weft: undyed linen; red, gold, and three shades of blue wool
8" x 6⅛" (20.3 cm x 16.2 cm)
Acquired in 1951 from Phocion Tano, Cairo
Exhibited: American Federation of Arts Loan Exhibition: "Abstract Art in Ancient Textiles," 1959-60; "Found in Egypt," Textile Museum, 1963
72.183

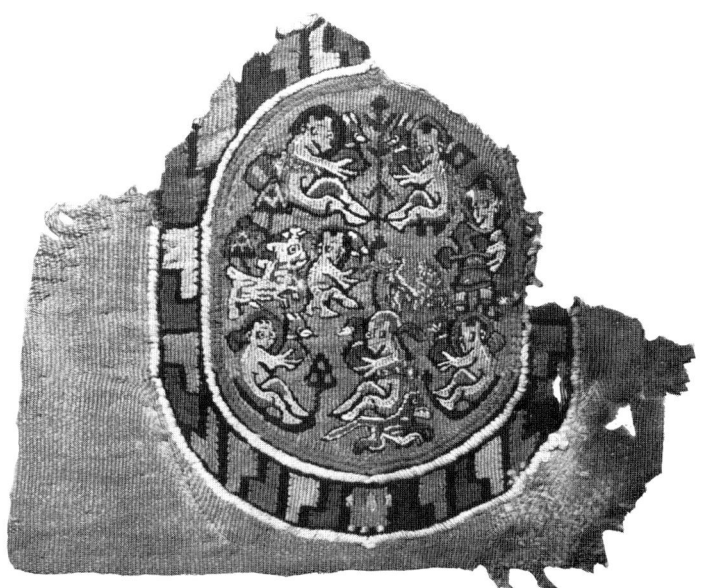

24 Tapestry decoration with an unidentified scene

Sixth century or later

This tapestry exemplifies the disintegration of classical form which is found in a large number of Late Roman and Early Byzantine tapestries. Further research is required to determine whether this phenomenon indicates a late date or whether it can be explained in terms of extreme provincialism alone. A tapestry identical to this one in both style and composition is in the Louvre (du Bourguet: *Catalogue des étoffes coptes*, no. G127).

Tapestry over one warp, slit and dovetailed; weft wrapping; eccentric wefts; plain weave ground
Warp: red wool
Weft: (tapestry) undyed, red, blue, green and ochre wool; (plain weave) red wool
8⅛" x 6⅝" (20.7 cm x 16.9 cm)
Acquired in 1940 from Phocion Tano, Cairo
72.90

23 Tunic with human and animal figures
Sixth century(?)

Tapestry over one warp, slit and dovetailed; weft wrapping; eccentric wefts; plain weave ground
Warp: undyed wool
Weft: (tapestry) undyed, red, orange, blue, green, purple and ochre wool; (plain weave) undyed wool
58½" x 27" (148.5 cm x 68.6 cm)
Acquired in 1935 from Phocion Tano, Cairo
72.61

25 Tunic decoration depicting the Judgment of Paris
Fourth century

Distinguishing features of this tapestry include the size and shape of the eyes, a predilection for awkward postures, and a considerable degree of naturalism in the treatment of drapery. A companion piece is in the Musée de l'Industrie in Saint-Gall (*Connaissance des Arts*, no. 359, Jan. 1982, p. 41). Other closely related works include Shurinova: *Coptic Textiles*, no. 5, and Wulff and Volbach: *Spätantike und koptische Stoffe*, no. 11452, pl. 67. A tapestry in the Metropolitan Museum, no. 90.5.837 (*Age of Spirituality*, cat. no. 121, p. 142) is similar in its treatment of eyes, postures, and floral background, but is generally more precise and assured. It may represent an earlier phase of the same style. The tapestry in Wulff and Volbach, 11452 mentioned above, has features in common with three other pieces in the Textile Museum, cat. nos. 26, 27 and 28. Further research will doubtless clarify the relation of the *Judgment of Paris* to these three works.

Tapestry over paired or triple warps, slit and dovetailed; weft wrapping; eccentric wefts; sewn to plain weave ground with triple wefts at regular intervals

Warp: undyed linen
Weft: undyed linen, purple wool
Plain weave: undyed linen
6⅝" x 5⅞" (17 cm x 15 cm) (tapestry only)
Acquired in 1950 from Phocion Tano, Cairo
Exhibited: Essen, Villa Hügel, 1953; Zürich, Kunsthaus 1963-64; Vienna, Akademie der bildenden Künste 1964; New York, Metropolitan Museum of Art 1977
Published: *Koptische Kunst*, Essen-Bredeney, 1963, cat. no. 290; *Koptische Kunst*, Zürich, 1963, cat. no. 258; *Frühchristliche und koptische Kunst*, Vienna, 1964, cat. no. 535; *Age of Spirituality*, New York, 1977, cat. no. 116, pp. 138-39
71.117

26 Tunic with mythological scenes in roundels

Fourth to fifth century

The larger medallions probably illustrate a scene from the story of Orestes and Iphigenia (K. Weitzmann in *Antike Kunst*, 7 (1964), pp. 42–47).

The figure style, leaf forms, and the use of a striated ground link this tunic to cat. nos. 27 and 28 (compare the leaves in no. 27B). Cat. nos. 25 and 29 may also be related. Other similar tapestries include Lewis: *Early Coptic Textiles*, pl. 43, and Matie and Liapunova: *Textiles of Coptic Egypt*, pls. 18.2 and 31.6.

Slit tapestry over paired or triple warps; weft wrapping; eccentric wefts; plain weave ground
Warp: undyed linen
Weft: (tapestry) undyed linen, purple wool; (plain weave) undyed linen
Dimensions as mounted (folded): 39½" x 34½" (104 cm x 87.5 cm); diameter of larger roundels: 3¼" (8.2 cm)
Acquired in 1940 from Phocion Tano, Cairo
Exhibited: New York, Cooper-Hewitt Museum (Special Opening Exhibit), 1963

Published: R. Berliner, "Remarks on Some Tapestries From Egypt," *Textile Museum Journal*, 1,4 (1965), pp. 23 ff.

71.72.

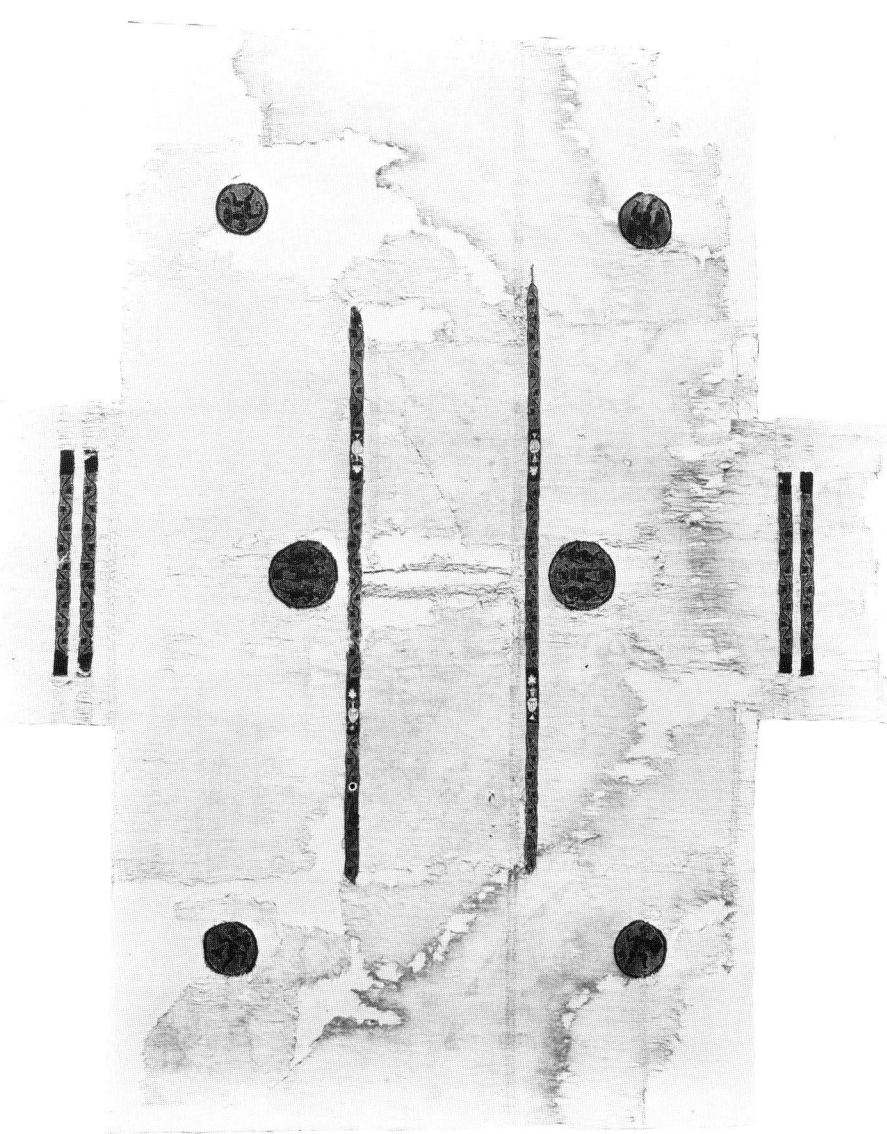

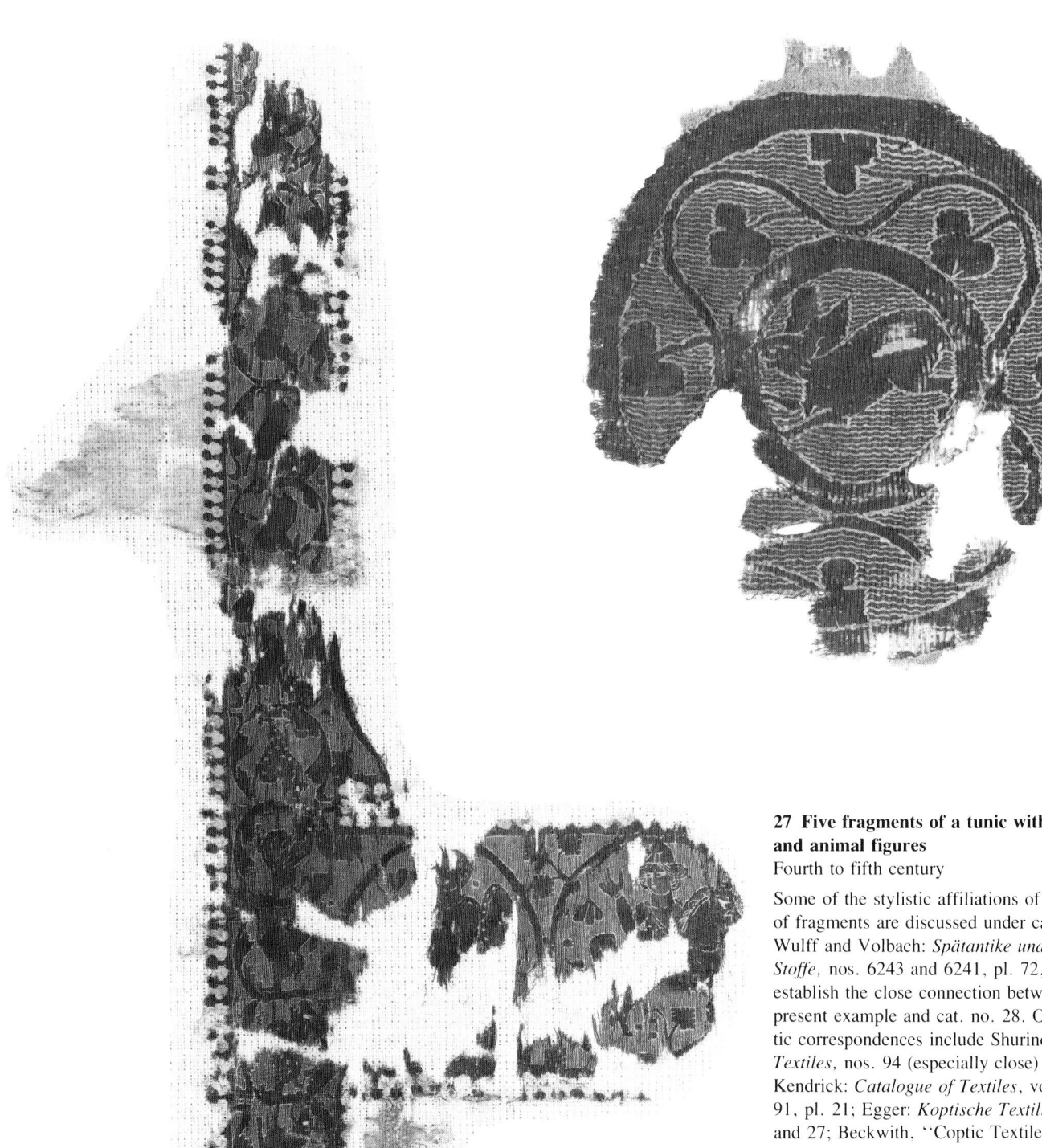

27 Five fragments of a tunic with human and animal figures
Fourth to fifth century

Some of the stylistic affiliations of this group of fragments are discussed under cat. no. 26. Wulff and Volbach: *Spätantike und koptische Stoffe,* nos. 6243 and 6241, pl. 72, together establish the close connection between the present example and cat. no. 28. Other stylistic correspondences include Shurinova: *Coptic Textiles,* nos. 94 (especially close) and 6; Kendrick: *Catalogue of Textiles,* vol. I, no. 91, pl. 21; Egger: *Koptische Textilien,* pls. 26 and 27; Beckwith, "Coptic Textiles," *CIBA Review,* 12:133 (August, 1959), p. 9; and Akashi: *Coptic Textiles,* vol. I, pl. 48 and vol. III, pl. 123.

Slit tapestry over paired or triple warps; weft wrapping; eccentric wefts; plain weave ground of exceptional fineness with bands of multiple wefts
Warp: undyed linen
Weft: (tapestry) undyed linen, purple wool; (plain weave) undyed linen
A. 13½" x 8" (34.4 cm x 20.3 cm)
B. 10" x 3⅝" (25.4 cm x 9.2 cm)
C. 18¼" x 5⅞" (46.3 cm x 15 cm)
D. Diameter 3" (7.6 cm)
E. 15½" x 7" (39.4 cm x 18 cm)
Acquired in 1953 from Michel Abemayor, New York
1961.22.29a-e

28 Square decoration from a tunic

Fourth to fifth century

The stylistic affiliations of this tapestry are discussed under cat. nos. 26 and 27. Further comparisons include Akashi: *Coptic Textiles*, vol. III, pl. 132; Matie and Liapunova: *Textiles of Coptic Egypt*, pl. 31.6; and Shurinova: *Coptic Textiles*, no. 46 (border of vines and vases).

Tapestry over paired or triple warps; weft wrapping; eccentric wefts; plain weave ground with paired wefts at intervals
Warp: undyed linen
Weft: (tapestry) undyed linen, purple wool; (plain weave) undyed linen
7½" x 7⅛" (19 cm x 18 cm)
Acquired in 1948 from James Pullen, Oakland
72.136

29 Tunic decoration with a scene of combat

The main panel depicts a figure on foot taking prisoner a mounted figure. Shurinova illustrates a similar scene, which she identifies as a combat between a Greek and an Amazon (Shurinova: *Coptic Textiles*, no. 7). In both cases the standing figure is male despite the rounded hips. In the present case the mounted figure seems to be wearing a short tunic of the kind associated with Amazons. The difference in size between the two figures may reflect a difference in sex, but it is so exaggerated that it is more likely a survival of the ancient Egyptian and Middle Eastern convention which made the victor by far the largest figure in a scene of battle. Stirrups were not yet in use when this tapestry was woven; compare the mounted figure of Alexander the Great in a tapestry of the seventh or eighth century in the Museum's collection (D. Shepherd, "Alexander, the Victorious Emperor," *Bulletin of the Cleveland Museum*, October 1971, pp. 245-250).

Slit tapestry over paired warps; weft wrapping; eccentric wefts; in a plain weave ground with triple wefts at irregular intervals
Warp: undyed linen
Weft: (tapestry) undyed linen, purple wool; (plain weave) undyed linen
Maximum dimensions: 12½" x 9¼" (31.8 cm x 23.5 cm)
Acquired in 1948 from James Pullen, Oakland
72.145

30 Medallion with a head of Dionysus
Fourth century

This tapestry is part of the same set as cat. nos. 31 and 32.

Tapestry over paired and triple warps in regular alternation, slit and dovetailed; weft wrapping; eccentric wefts
Warp: undyed linen
Weft: undyed linen, purple and tan wool
12¼″ x 10⅞″ (31 cm x 27.5 cm)
Acquired in 1947 from Phocion Tano, Cairo
Exhibited: The Hill School, 1950; Hartford, Wadsworth Atheneum, and Baltimore, Museum of Art, 1951-52; Essen, Villa Hügel, 1963; Zürich, Kunsthaus, 1963-64; Vienna, Akademie der bildenden Künste, 1964; Paris, Petit Palais, 1964; New York, Metropolitan Museum of Art, 1977
Published: A.C. Weibel: *2000 Years of Tapestry Weaving*, Hartford, 1951, cat. no. 4, pl. 1; *Koptische Kunst*, Essen-Bredeney, 1963, cat. no. 263; *Koptische Kunst*, Zürich, 1963, cat. no. 293; *Frühchristliche und koptische Kunst*, Vienna, 1964, cat. no. 512; *l'Art copte*, Paris, 1964, cat. no. 258; W.F. Volbach: *Early Decorative Textiles*, London and New York, 1969, p. 20, pl. 7; *Age of Spirituality*, New York, 1977, no. 120, p. 41
71.106

32 Medallion with a head of Dionysus
Fourth century

This tapestry, which is pieced together from four fragments, is part of the same set as cat. nos. 30 and 31.

Tapestry over paired and triple warps in regular alternation, slit and dovetailed; weft wrapping; eccentric wefts; plain weave ground
Warp: undyed linen
Weft: (tapestry) undyed linen, purple and tan wool; (plain weave) undyed linen
13⅛″ x 10⅝″ (34 cm x 27 cm)
Acquired in 1947 from Phocion Tano, Cairo
71.108

31 Medallion with a head of Dionysus
Fourth century

Cat. nos. 30 and 32 belong to the same set, which must originally have adorned a large curtain or cover. It is not known how many medallions made up the complete set.

Tapestry over paired and triple warps in regular alternation, slit and dovetailed; weft wrapping; eccentric wefts; plain weave ground
Warp: undyed linen
Weft: (tapestry) undyed linen, purple and tan wool; (plain weave) undyed linen
12¼″ x 10″ (31 cm x 25.5 cm)
Acquired in 1947 from Phocion Tano, Cairo
Exhibited: The Hill School, 1950; Essen, Villa Hügel, 1963; Zürich, Kunstahus, 1963-64; Vienna, Akademie der bildenden Künste, 1964; Paris, Petit Palais, 1964; Washington, D.C., Textile Museum, 1976; "Myth and Gospel: Art of Coptic Egypt," Newark Museum, 1977-78
Published: *Koptische Kunst*, Essen-Bredeney, 1963, cat. no. 264, color pl. 4; *Koptische Kunst*, Zürich, 1963, cat. no. 240, color pl. 7; *Frühchristliche und koptische Kunst*, Vienna, 1964, cat. no. 513; *l'Art copte*, Paris, 1964, cat. no. 259; L. Mackie and A.P. Rowe: *Masterpieces in the Textile Museum*, Washington, 1976, cover
71.107

33 Tunic decoration with hunting scenes
Fifth or sixth century

For another tapestry in a similar style see Apostolakis: *Ta Koptika Huphasmata*, no. 1732, fig. 87. There is also a resemblance between this tapestry and fifth-century woolen fabrics woven on a drawloom; see for example a textile in the Philadelphia Museum of Art, no. 33-50-1 (A.C. Weibel: *Two Thousand Years of Textiles*, no. 37).

Tapestry over one warp, slit and dovetailed; weft wrapping; eccentric wefts; plain weave ground
Warp: ochre wool
Weft: (tapestry) tan, green, and dark blue wool; (plain weave) ochre wool
8¾" x 8¼" (22.3 cm x 21 cm)
Acquired in 1932 from Phocion Tano, Cairo
72.30

34 Tunic decoration with a hunting scene
Fifth century(?)

The tapestry depicts a hunter, accompanied by a dog, spearing a large animal, probably a lion. The same theme, complete with vase border, is treated in a different style in a tapestry in the Louvre (du Bourguet: *Catalogue des étoffes coptes*, no. C22).

Tapestry over paired and triple warps, slit and dovetailed; weft wrapping; eccentric wefts; sewn to plain weave ground
Warp: undyed linen
Weft: undyed linen, purple wool
Plain weave: undyed linen
4½" x 3¾" (10.8 cm x 9.5 cm) (tapestry only)
Acquired in 1968 from Christian Grand, Zürich
1968.8.8

35 Tunic decoration with animals
Sixth century
Tapestry over one warp, slit and dovetailed; weft wrapping; eccentric wefts
Warp: dark blue-green wool
Weft: undyed wool, red wool
11¼" x 10⅝" (28.5 cm x 27.5 cm)
Acquired in 1947 from Phocion Tano, Cairo
71.102

36 Roundel from a tunic
Fourth or fifth century
Slit tapestry over one warp; weft wrapping; eccentric wefts; plain weave ground
Warp: undyed linen
Weft: (tapestry) undyed linen, pinkish-red wool; (plain weave) undyed linen
3⅛" x 3" (8.5 cm x 7.5 cm)
Acquired in 1928 from Paul Mallon, Paris
Exhibited: "Found in Egypt," Textile Museum, 1963
71.19

37 Fragment with mythological figures
Fifth century
Three erotes hold a long garland. Of the other figures, one is mounted on a mythical seahorse or hippocamp, and the remainder are shown in attitudes which suggest that they are swimming.

Tapestry over one warp, slit and dovetailed; weft wrapping; eccentric wefts; plain weave ground
Warp: undyed wool
Weft: (tapestry) undyed linen, purple wool; (plain weave) undyed wool
16⅜" x 5½" (41.5 cm x 14 cm)
Acquired in 1930 from Khawam Brothers, Cairo

(from the collection of Vladimir Simkhovitch, New York)
Exhibited: Brooklyn Museum, 1941
Published: *Pagan and Christian Egypt*, Brooklyn, 1941, no. 208; D. Levi: *Antioch Mosaic Pavements*, Princeton, 1947, vol. I, p. 267 and fig. 105
71.26

38 Tunic decoration with a female figure flanked by animals
Sixth century(?)
The same theme is treated in a less precise style in a tapestry in the Louvre (du Bourguet: *Catalogue des étoffes coptes*, no. G44).
Slit tapestry over one warp; weft wrapping; eccentric wefts; plain weave ground
Warp: undyed wool
Weft: (tapestry) undyed wool, purple wool; (plain weave) undyed wool
9" x 4½" (23.2 cm x 11.5 cm)
Acquired in 1948 from Phocion Tano, Cairo
Exhibited: "Found in Egypt," Textile Museum, 1963
72.126

39 Roundel from a tunic
Fifth or sixth century(?)
The halo and scepter which adorn the central bust are associated with rulers, as well as with angels, personifications, and some mythological figures (cf. cat. no. 5). In the absence of other attributes, e.g. the mural crown of a city goddess or *tuchē*, it is not possible to identify the subject with certainty.
Tapestry over plied warps, slit and dovetailed; weft wrapping; eccentric wefts
Warp: undyed linen
Weft: red wool, yellow wool
Maximum diameter: 9⅝" (24.5 cm)
Acquired in 1940 from Phocion Tano, Cairo
71.71

40 Tunic decoration with an eagle
Fifth century or later
Similar tapestries include Zaloscer: *Ägyptische Wirkereien*, pl. 8; Shurinova: *Coptic Textiles*, no. 111.
Tapestry over paired warps, slit and dovetailed; weft wrapping; eccentric wefts; plain weave ground
Warp: undyed linen
Weft: (tapestry) undyed linen, dark blue wool; (plain weave) undyed linen
9⅞" x 6¾" (25 cm x 17 cm)
Acquired in 1953 from Phocion Tano, Cairo
71.128

41 Tunic decoration (?) with victories holding wreaths

Fifth century(?)
This tapestry is identical in style to a larger fragment in the Ashmolean Museum in Oxford (no. 1941.1133; illustrated in Lubell: *Textile Collections*, vol. 2, p. 103). For the theme of victories holding up wreaths or shields, cf. a fresco of the second century A.D. from Palmyra (C.H. Kraeling, "Color Photographs of the Painting in the Tomb of the Three Brothers at Palmyra," *Annales archéologiques de Syrie*, 11-12, Damascus, 1961-62, pl. 6).
Tapestry over one warp, slit and dovetailed; weft wrapping; eccentric wefts

Warp: undyed wool
Weft: undyed linen, blue wool, pale purple wool
9½" x 7⅞" (24 cm x 20 cm)
Acquired in 1944 from Vladimir Simkhovitch, New York
Exhibited: Brooklyn Museum, 1941
Published: *Pagan and Christian Egypt*, Brooklyn, 1941, no. 209
71.84

42 Fragment of a curtain or hanging
Fifth century(?)

This tapestry belongs to a group of large hangings in which boldly drawn figures on a plain ground are separated by vertical panels containing smaller figures or floral ornament. A tapestry in the British Museum is the best-preserved example of this group, with two large figures and three separating panels (Wessel: *Coptic Art*, fig. 118). Still larger pieces may have been made.

In terms of style and arrangement the closest parallel to the Textile Museum's tapestry is furnished by a tapestry in the Louvre (*l'Art copte*, Paris, 1964, cat. no. 176). Other examples of the same type include Wulff and Volbach: *Spätantike und koptische Stoffe*, no. 9230, pl. 44; *Exposition d'art copte* (Cairo, Société d'Archéologie Copte, 1944), no. 45, pl. 4; Museum of Fine Arts, Boston, no. 06.2385.

For the bold, simple drawing of the main figure cf. du Bourguet: *Catalogue des étoffes coptes*, nos. B17 and B18. For the side panels cf. Matie and Liapunova: *Textiles of Coptic Egypt*, pl. 22.4 (virtually identical) and pl. 38.5; Wulff and Volbach, no. 6235, pl. 51.

Cat. no. 43 is almost certainly from a hanging of the same type, as is cat. no. 13: cf. Wulff and Volbach, no. 9230, pl. 44.

Tapestry over paired or triple wefts, slit and dovetailed; weft wrapping; eccentric wefts; plain weave ground with bands of paired or triple warps
Warp: undyed linen
Weft: (tapestry) undyed linen; purple, green, red, pink, yellow and blue wool; (plain weave) undyed linen
48″ x 38¾″ (121.8 cm x 98.5 cm)
Acquired in 1941 from Paul Mallon, Paris
71.79

43 Fragment of a curtain or hanging with a winged figure

Fifth century (?)

This fragment is probably from the central panel of a large hanging like cat. no. 42. Close parallels for the figure style include du Bourguet: *Catalogue des étoffes coptes,* no. B17, and Wulff and Volbach: *Spätantike und koptische Stoffe,* no. 9230, pl. 44.

Slit tapestry over paired or tripled warps; weft wrapping; eccentric wefts; plain weave ground
Warp: undyed linen
Weft: (tapestry) undyed linen, red, ochre, and dark blue wool; (plain weave) undyed linen
Maximum dimensions: 14⅝" x 10¼" (36.2 cm x 26 cm)
Acquired in 1948 from Phocion Tano, Cairo
Exhibited: "Abstract Art in Ancient Textiles," A.F.A. loan exhibition, 1959-60
72.124

44 Fragment with a dancing female figure

Fifth century (?)

This fragment probably formed part of an interlace border with alternating square and circular compartments containing figures. For such a border cf. a textile at Dumbarton Oaks, no. 73.7. For the figure style cf. Thompson: *Coptic Textiles in the Brooklyn Museum*, no. 20.

Tapestry over paired warps, slit and dovetailed; weft wrapping; eccentric wefts
Warp: undyed linen
Weft: undyed linen, purple wool, tan wool
8⅞″ x 8½″ (22.5 cm x 21.5 cm)
Acquired in 1947 from Phocion Tano, Cairo
Exhibited: "Found in Egypt," Textile Museum, 1963
71.100

45 Tunic decoration with figures in an arcade

Fifth century(?)

This tapestry forms a coherent stylistic group with cat. nos. 46, 47 and 52, and probably also 48 and 49. For other pieces belonging to the same group see Peter: *Textilien aus Ägypten*, nos. 15 and 16, and du Bourguet: *Catalogue des étoffes coptes*, no. C28.

Tapestry over paired or triple warps; weft wrapping; eccentric wefts; plain weave ground
Warp: undyed linen
Weft: (tapestry) undyed linen, purple, brown, green and red wool; (plain weave) undyed linen
16¼″ x 13⅞″ (41.4 cm x 35.3 cm)
Acquired in 1935 from Phocion Tano, Cairo
71I.26

46 Tunic decoration with figures in an arcade

Fifth century (?)

For the stylistic affiliations of this tapestry see cat. no. 45.

Slit tapestry over paired or triple warps; weft wrapping; eccentric wefts; plain weave ground
Warp: undyed linen
Weft: (tapestry) undyed linen, purple, red, green and rust wool; (plain weave) undyed linen
14⅞" x 12¾" (37.8 cm x 32.5 cm)
Acquired in 1935 from Phocion Tano, Cairo
Exhibited: Brooklyn Museum, 1941; "5000 Years of Fibers and Fabrics," Brooklyn Museum, 1946; The Hill School, 1950
Published: *Pagan and Christian Egypt*, Brooklyn, 1941, cat. no. 210
711.30

47 Tunic decoration with a nereid mounted on a mythical sea-creature

Fifth century (?)

For the stylistic affiliations of this tapestry see cat. no. 45.

Slit tapestry over paired or triple warps; weft wrapping; eccentric wefts; plain weave ground
Warp: undyed linen
Weft: (tapestry) undyed linen; purple, brown, red and green wool; (plain weave) undyed linen
13½" x 11⅞" (34.4 cm x 30.2 cm)
Acquired in 1960 from Christian Grand, Zürich
Exhibited: "Found in Egypt," Textile Museum, 1963
1960.20.7

48 *Clavus* fragment with animals and human busts
Fifth century (?)
For the stylistic affiliations of this tapestry see cat. no. 45.

Tapestry over paired and triple warps in regular alternation, slit and dovetailed; weft wrapping; eccentric wefts; plain weave ground
Warp: undyed linen

Weft: (tapestry) undyed linen, purple wool, rust wool; (plain weave) undyed linen
34⅝" x 14¼" (88 cm x 36 cm)
Acquired in 1935 from Phocion Tano, Cairo
Exhibited: "Found in Egypt," Textile Museum, 1963
71.60

49 Tunic decoration with animals
Fifth century (?)
For the stylistic affiliations of this tapestry see cat. no. 45. Other pieces which it closely resembles include the following: Akashi: *Coptic Textiles*, vol. III, pls. 103B and 122 (almost identical); Wulff and Volbach: *Spätantike und koptische Stoffe*, nos. 11450, pl. 55, 11442 and 11443, pl. 79; du Bourguet: *Catalogue des étoffes coptes*, no. D94.

Slit tapestry over paired or triple warps; weft wrapping; eccentric wefts; plain weave ground
Warp: undyed linen

Weft: (tapestry) undyed linen, purple wool; (plain weave) undyed linen
10⅞" x 5⅛" (27.7 cm x 13 cm)
Acquired in 1939 from Phocion Tano, Cairo
71.67

50 Tunic decoration (?) with lion and human bust in roundels
Fifth century

Tapestry over one warp, slit and dovetailed; weft wrapping; eccentric wefts
Warp: undyed wool
Weft: undyed wool, purple wool
11¼" x 2¾" (28.5 cm x 7 cm)
Acquired in 1928 from Hagop Kevorkian, New York
71.16

51 Fragment of a border with dancing figures
Fifth century (?)

The style of this tapestry is similar but not identical to that of cat. no. 45. Other close analogies include the following: Toll: *Coptic Textiles*, no. 21, pl. 3 (figure style and shape of frames); Shurinova: *Coptic Textiles*, no. 5; du Bourguet: *Catalogue des étoffes coptes*, nos. C30 (shape of frame), C32 and C33 (figure style); Wulff and Volbach: *Spätantike und koptische Stoffe*, no. 6813, pl. 56 (figure style and floral background); Matie and Liapunova: *Textiles of Coptic Egypt*, pl. 21.3.

Tapestry over paired or triple warps, slit and dovetailed; weft wrapping; eccentric wefts; plain weave ground
Warp: undyed linen
Weft: (tapestry) undyed linen; brownish-purple, mustard, red and reddish-brown wool; (plain weave) undyed linen
15" x 6¼" (38 cm x 16 cm)
Acquired in 1936 from Phocion Tano, Cairo
71.62

52 Tunic decoration with a rider
Fifth century (?)

On the rider theme see Kitzinger: "The Horse and Lion Tapestry," p. 35, and Lewis: "The Iconography of the Coptic Horseman." Similar representations of the subject include a tapestry at Dumbarton Oaks, no. 73.7; du Bourguet: *Catalogue des étoffes coptes*, no. C29; Wulff and Volbach: *Spätantike und koptische Stoffe*, no. 6729, pl. 69.
For the stylistic affiliations of this tapestry see cat. no. 45.

Tapestry over paired or triple warps, slit and dovetailed; weft wrapping; eccentric wefts; plain weave ground
Warp: undyed linen
Weft: (tapestry) undyed linen, purple, brown, green and red wool; (plain weave) undyed linen
9½" x 8⅝" (24 cm x 22 cm)
Acquired in 1935 from Phocion Tano, Cairo
71.61

53 Tunic decoration with a rider
Fifth century

For the style and the arrangement of elements cf. du Bourguet: *Catalogue des étoffes coptes,* no. D86, and Wulff and Volbach: *Spätantike und koptische Stoffe,* no. 6729, pl. 69.

Tapestry over one warp, slit and dovetailed; weft wrapping; eccentric wefts
Warp: undyed wool
Weft: undyed linen, purple wool
9⅝" x 8½" (24.5 cm x 21.5 cm)
Acquired in 1927 from the Anderson Galleries, New York (from the sale of the Kevorkian Collection)
Exhibited: "Found in Egypt," Textile Museum, 1963
Published: The Anderson Galleries, New York: *The H. Kevorkian Collection of Near and Far Eastern Art,* 1927, no. 55 (illus.); S. Lewis: "The Iconography of the Coptic Horseman in Byzantine Egypt," pp. 30-31 and fig. 7)
71.6

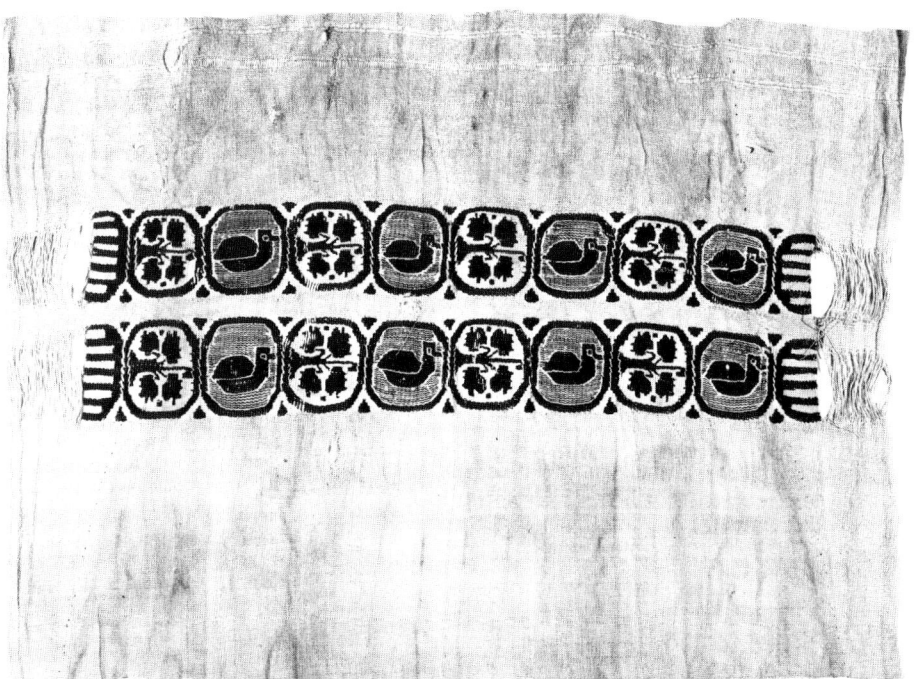

54 Tunic decoration with ducks and trees in repeated frames
Fifth or sixth century

Several published tapestries are clearly from the same workshop. Kybalova: *Coptic Textiles,* pl. 38, and Wulff and Volbach: *Spätantike und koptische Stoffe,* nos. 9683 and 9657, pl. 64, probably represent an earlier stage in its development. Du Bourguet: *Catalogue des étoffes coptes,* nos. D61, D62 and D63, and Akashi: *Coptic Textiles,* vol. I, pl. 30, represent the same approximate stage as the piece illustrated here. Du Bourguet, no. E2 is probably slightly later.

Tapestry over paired warps, slit and dovetailed; weft wrapping; eccentric wefts; plain weave ground with rows of triple wefts along one edge of the fragment
Warp: Undyed linen
Weft: (tapestry) undyed linen, purple wool; (plain weave) undyed linen
12⅞" x 9¼" (32.5 cm x 23.5 cm)
Acquired in 1954 from Phocion Tano, Cairo
71.133

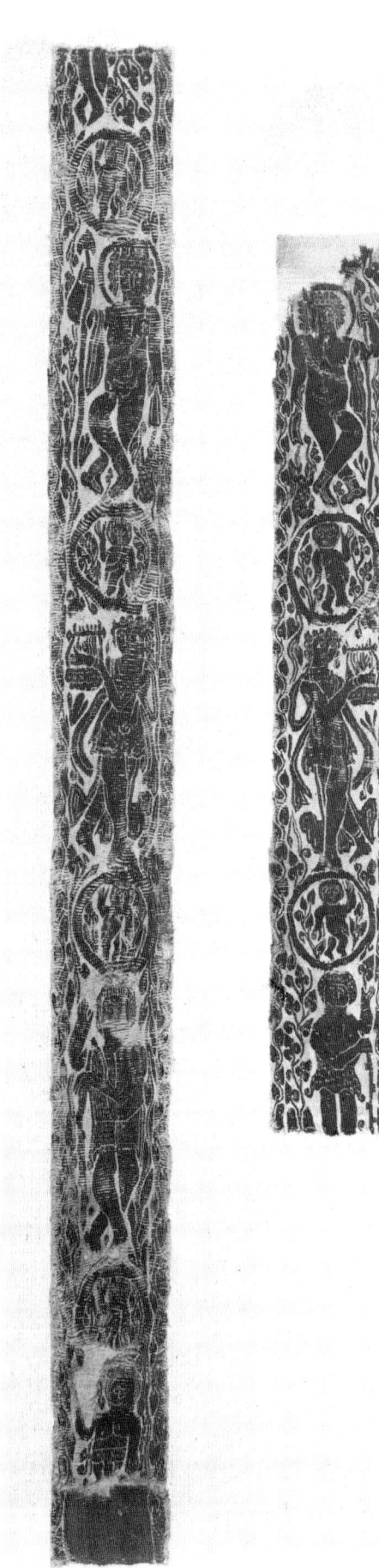

55 Pair of *clavi* with Dionysus and other figures

Late fourth or early fifth century(?)

For the theme see V. Lenzen: "The Triumph of Dionysos on Textiles of Late Antique Egypt," *University of California Publications in Classical Archaeology*, 5 (1960), pp. 1-38. A tapestry in the Hermitage is in an identical style; see Matie and Liapunova: *Textiles of Coptic Egypt*, pl. 21.2. For other stylistic parallels see Kybalova: *Coptic Textiles*, pl. 20, and du Bourguet: *Catalogue des étoffes coptes*, no. B19.

Tapestry over triple warps, slit and dovetailed; weft wrapping; eccentric wefts
Warp: undyed linen
Weft: undyed linen, purple wool
25½" x 2⅛" (65 cm x 5.5 cm)
15⅛" x 2⅛" (38.5 cm x 5.5 cm)
Acquired in 1932 from Herbert Weissberger, New York
Exhibited: Brooklyn Museum, 1941
Published: *Pagan and Christian Egypt*, Brooklyn, 1941, no. 187 (illus.)
71.38

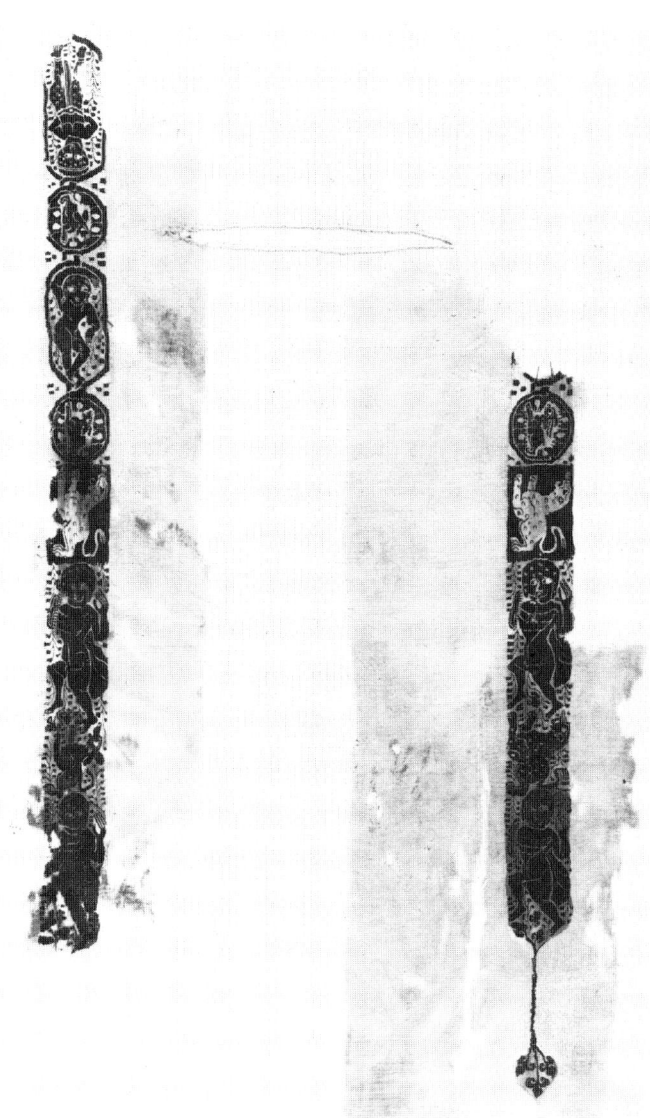

56 Pair of fragmentary *clavi* with human and animal figures

Fifth century (?)

For framing medallions of similar shape see Volbach: *Spätantike und frühmittelalterliche Stoffe*, no. 159, pl. 5; Kybalova: *Coptic Textiles*, fig. 37; Matie and Liapunova: *Textiles of Coptic Egypt*, pl. 16. For a complete tunic with similar though not identical decoration see Dimand: "Coptic Tunics," fig. 4.

Tapestry over one warp, slit and dovetailed; weft wrapping; eccentric wefts; plain weave ground with triple wefts at regular (?) intervals

Warp: undyed wool

Weft: (tapestry) undyed linen, purple wool; (plain weave) undyed linen

19⅜" x 3¾" (49.3 cm x 9.7 cm)
18⅜" x 6⅜" (46.7 cm x 16.3 cm)

Exhibited: "Found in Egypt," Textile Museum, 1963

72.132

57 Tunic decoration (shoulder square and *clavus*) with human and animal figures

Fifth or sixth century

For a tapestry of identical style see Baginski and Tidhar: *Textiles from Egypt*, no. 69.

Tapestry over one warp, slit and dovetailed; weft wrapping; eccentric wefts; plain weave ground; a band of countered extra-weft wrapping between *clavus* and shoulder square

Warp: undyed wool

Weft: (tapestry) undyed wool, dark blue wool; (plain weave) undyed wool

19½" x 10" (49.5 cm x 25.5 cm)

Acquired in 1951 from Michel Abemayor, New York

71.122

58 Fragment of a *clavus*
Fifth century (?)

A tapestry of identical style is in the Hermitage (Matie and Liapunova: *Textiles of Coptic Egypt*, pl. 23.4). Other, similar works include Shurinova: *Coptic Textiles*, no. 44, and Wulff and Volbach: *Spätantike und koptische Stoffe*, no. 9658, pl. 53.

Tapestry over paired and triple warps in regular alternation, slit and dovetailed; weft wrapping; eccentric wefts; plain weave ground with triple wefts at intervals

Warp: undyed linen
Weft: (tapestry) undyed linen, purple wool; (plain weave) undyed linen
16″ x 3″ (40.5 cm x 7.5 cm)
Acquired in 1952 from Joseph Costa, New York
71.124

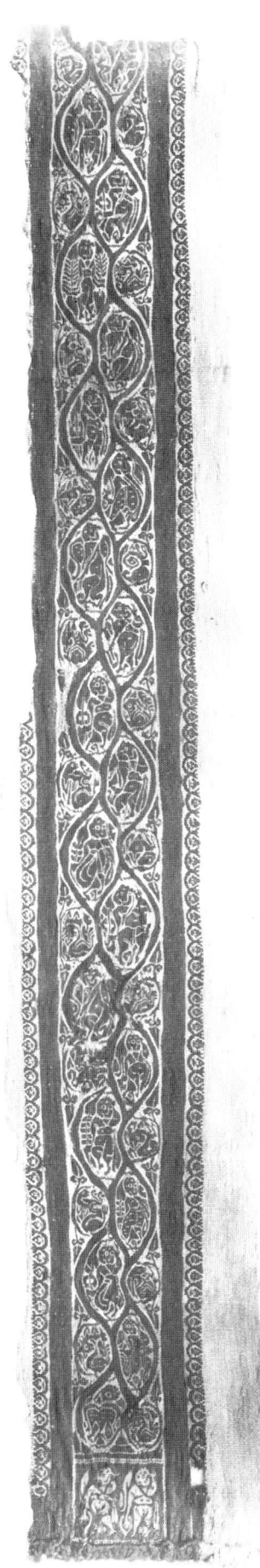

59 Tunic decoration (?) with figures in multiple frames
Sixth century (?)

The irregular, offset compartments which enclose the figures are probably derived from a vine rinceau, but the arrangement is uncommon and may be confined to a single workshop. Other examples include cat. no. 60 and du Bourguet: *Catalogue des étoffes coptes*, nos. H110-H113. Peter: *Textilien aus Ägypten*, no. 26 uses the same motif with a somewhat different figure style; this may be an exception, or it may represent an earlier phase in the development of the workshop. Cat. no. 61, du Bourguet, no. E39, and Peter, no. 55 are identical in style to the present work, but use a different framing pattern.

No. 59 and related works are among the few successful ornamental treatments of the human figure in Late Roman weaving. The figures themselves are so fragmented as to be almost unrecognizable. However, when combined with the nervous, abrupt rhythm of the framing pattern they create an effect which is both graceful and dynamic. For related figure styles cf. Kendrick: *Catalogue of Textiles*, vol. I, no. 90, pl. 20; du Bourguet, no. E39; and perhaps also cat. no. 39.

Technical information not available, but cf. cat. nos. 60 and 61
36" x 6½" (92 cm x 16 cm)
Acquired in 1935 from Phocion Tano, Cairo
72.64

60 Tunic decoration (?) with figures in multiple frames
Sixth century (?)
The style and affiliations of this tapestry are discussed under cat. no. 59.
Tapestry over one warp, slit and dovetailed; weft wrapping; eccentric wefts; plain weave ground
Warp: undyed wool
Weft: (tapestry) undyed wool, dark blue wool; (plain weave) undyed wool
10¼" x 8⅜" (26 cm x 21.2 cm)
Acquired in 1932 from Phocion Tano, Cairo
72.32

61 Roundel from a tunic

Sixth century (?)

The style and affiliations of this tapestry are discussed under cat. no. 59.

Tapestry over one warp, slit and dovetailed; weft wrapping; eccentric wefts; plain weave ground
Warp: undyed wool
Weft: (tapestry) undyed wool, dark blue wool; (plain weave) undyed wool
Maximum dimensions of fragment: 8¼" x 7¼" (20.8 cm x 18.6 cm)
Acquired in 1935 from Phocion Tano, Cairo
72.63

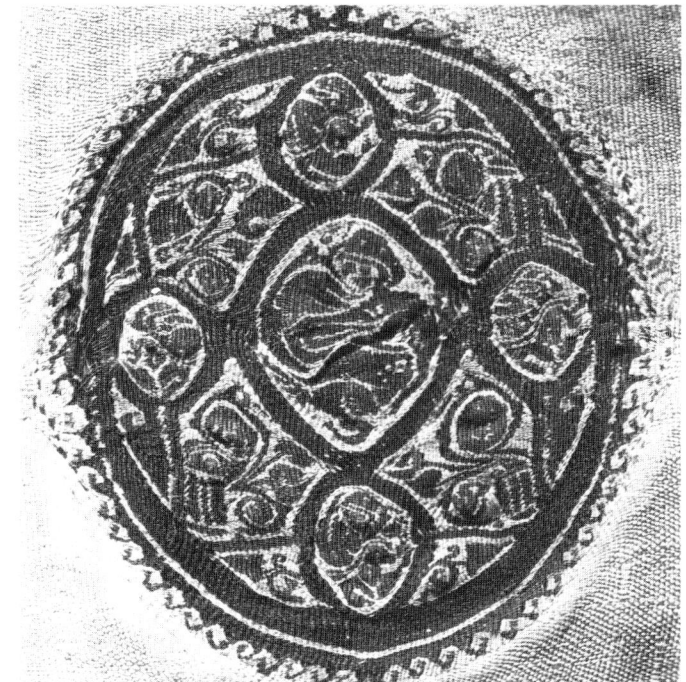

62 Tunic decoration (?) in the form of a leaf

Fourth to fifth century

For similar examples see Lewis: *Early Coptic Textiles*, pl. 18; du Bourguet: *Catalogues des étoffes coptes*, no. D26; Akashi: *Coptic Textiles*, vol. II, pl. 95. It is interesting to note that the same basic form can be made to represent a tree instead of a leaf. Examples include du Bourguet, no. D28, and Kybalova: *Coptic Textiles*, figs. 75 and 79.

Slit tapestry over paired or triple warps; weft wrapping; eccentric wefts; plain weave ground
Warp: undyed linen
Weft: (tapestry) undyed linen, purple wool, wool-linen (purple-undyed); (plain weave) undyed linen
8¾" x 8¾" (22 cm x 22 cm)
Acquired in 1952 from Joseph Costa, New York
71.123

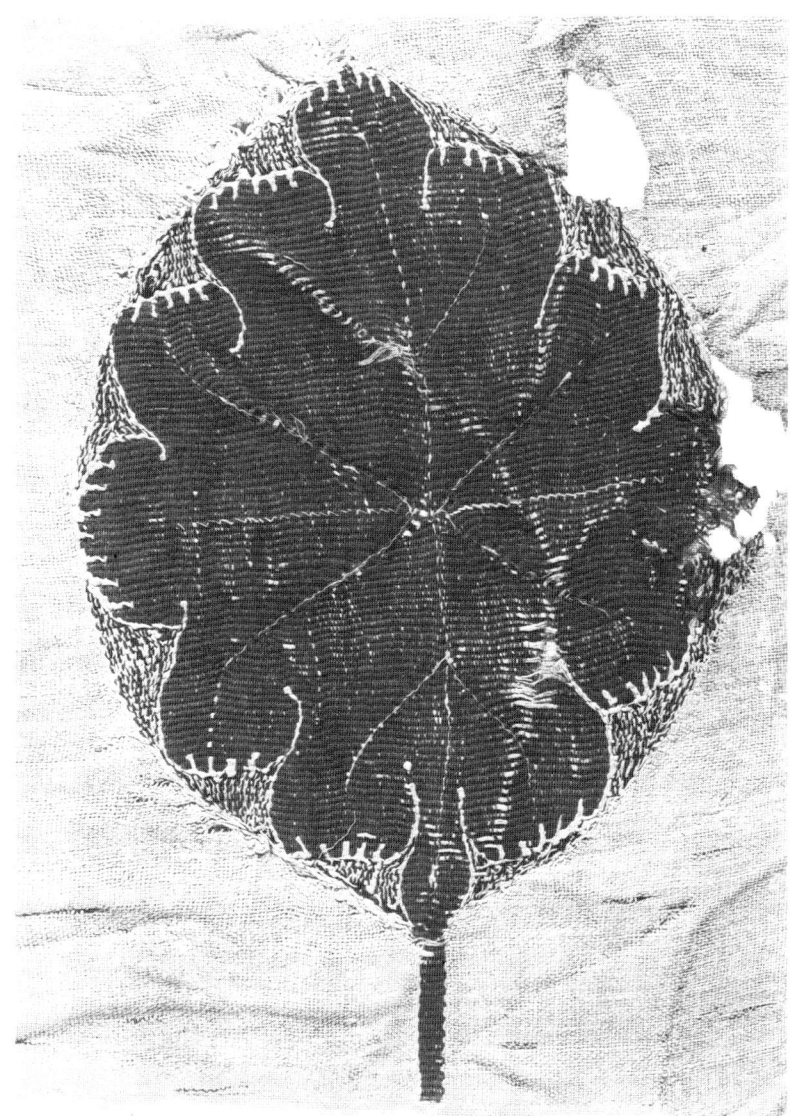

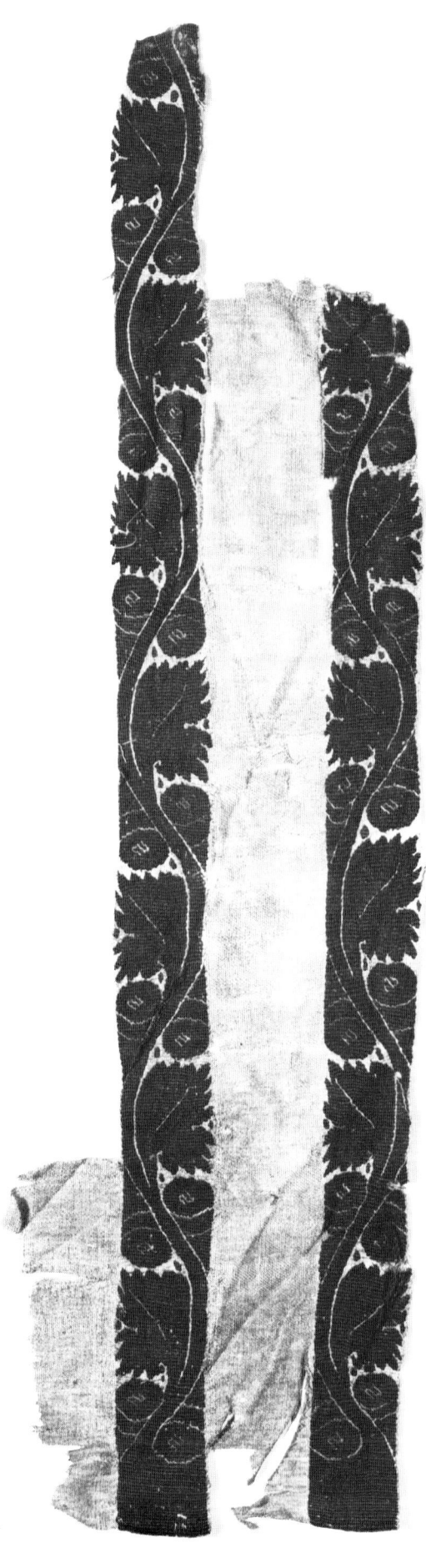

63 Fragment of a border (?) with a vine motif

Late fourth or early fifth century

This double strip of tapestry seems unusually broad for a *clavus*, though this may have been its function. Perhaps it was part of the border of a tunic, or of a shawl, cover or shroud (cf. cat. no. 99). Examples of similar vine ornament are illustrated in Renner: *Die koptischen Stoffe*, no. 9, pl. 8; Shurinova: *Coptic Textiles*, no. 24; du Bourguet: *Catalogue des étoffes coptes*, no. A20.

Tapestry over paired warps, slit and dovetailed; weft wrapping; eccentric wefts; plain weave ground
Warp: undyed linen
Weft: (tapestry) undyed linen, purple wool; (plain weave) undyed linen
25¼" x 7¼" (64 cm x 18.5 cm)
Acquired in 1947 from Phocion Tano, Cairo
71.101

64 Border with birds and stylized vines

Late fourth or early fifth century (?)

For other borders combining bands of tapestry with weft-loop pile, cf. cat. nos. 69 and 84. Such borders were used in curtains or large furniture covers.

Slit tapestry over paired and triple warps in regular alternation; weft wrapping; eccentric wefts; plain weave ground with supplementary wefts and weft-loops at regular intervals

Warp: undyed linen
Weft: (tapestry) undyed linen, purple wool; (plain weave and loops) undyed linen
26⅜" x 15⅜" (67 cm x 39 cm)
Acquired in 1944 from Robert McClenahan, Philadelphia
Exhibited: "Found in Egypt," Textile Museum, 1963
71.87

65 Tunic sleeve decoration (?) with animals in a vine rinceau

Fifth or sixth century

Tapestry over one warp, slit and dovetailed; weft wrapping; eccentric wefts
Warp: undyed wool
Weft: undyed wool, purple wool
10½" x 4" (26.7 cm x 9.9 cm)
Acquired in 1964 from Royal Athena Galleries, New York
1964.16.5

66 Tunic with floral decoration

Fifth century

A similar plant motif appears in a border in a tapestry in the Louvre (du Bourguet: *Catalogue des étoffes coptes*, no. D108).

Slit tapestry over one warp; weft wrapping; eccentric wefts; plain weave ground

Warp: undyed linen

Weft: (tapestry) undyed linen, purple or blue wool; (plain weave) undyed linen

54½" x 40" (137.8 cm x 101.6 cm)

71.73

67 Tunic decoration (?) with an inhabited vine motif

Late fourth or early fifth century

Many tapestries related to this one are cited under cat. no. 68. Others include Lewis: *Early Coptic Textiles*, pl. 30; Matie and Liapunova: *Textiles of Coptic Egypt*, pl. 27.3; Shurinova: *Coptic Textiles*, nos. 98, 99 and 100.

Tapestry over one warp, slit and dovetailed; weft wrapping; eccentric wefts; plain weave ground

Warp: undyed wool

Weft: (tapestry) undyed linen, purple wool; (plain weave) undyed wool

7" x 5⅛" (17.7 cm x 13 cm)

Acquired in 1932 from Phocion Tano, Cairo

Exhibited: "Found in Egypt," Textile Museum, 1963

Published: Riefstahl, A.F.A. Loan, 1933, p. 5, n. 5

71.49

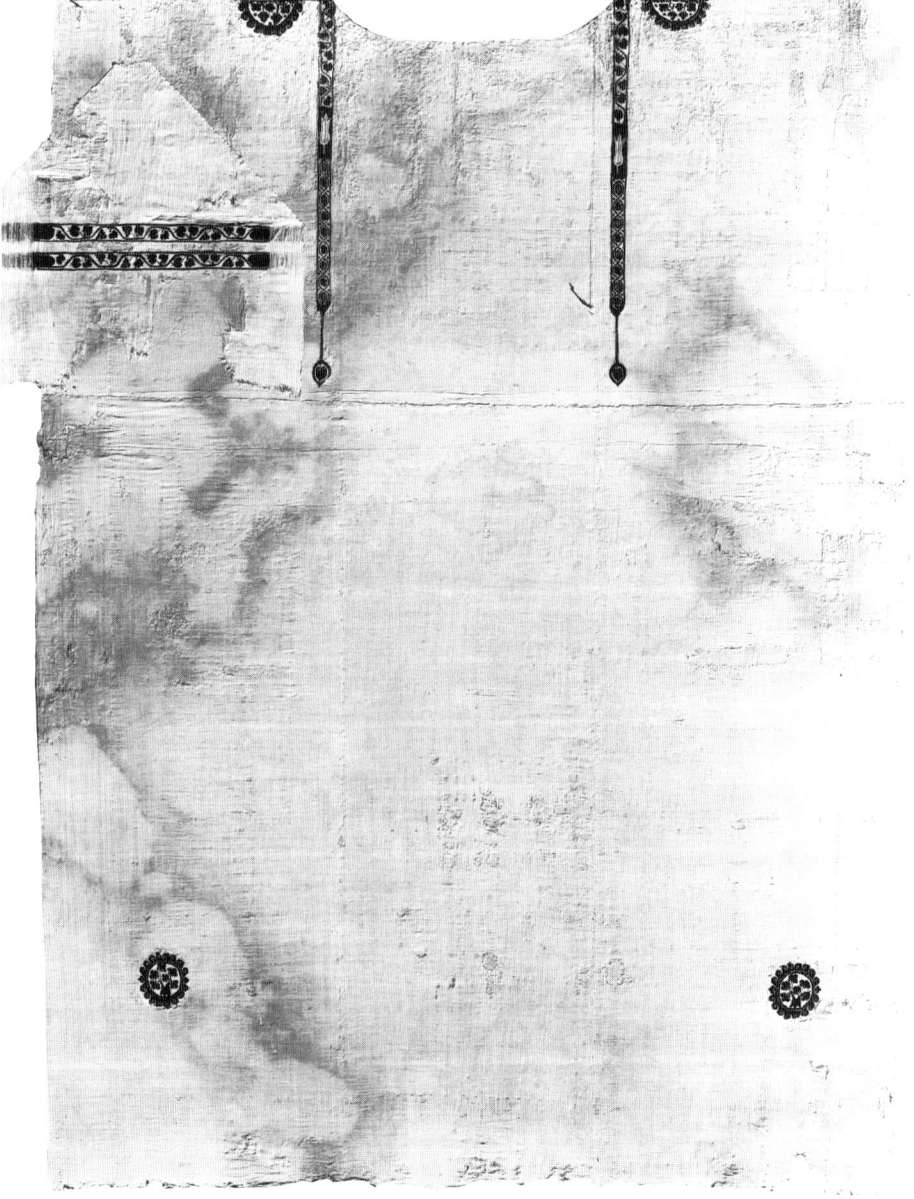

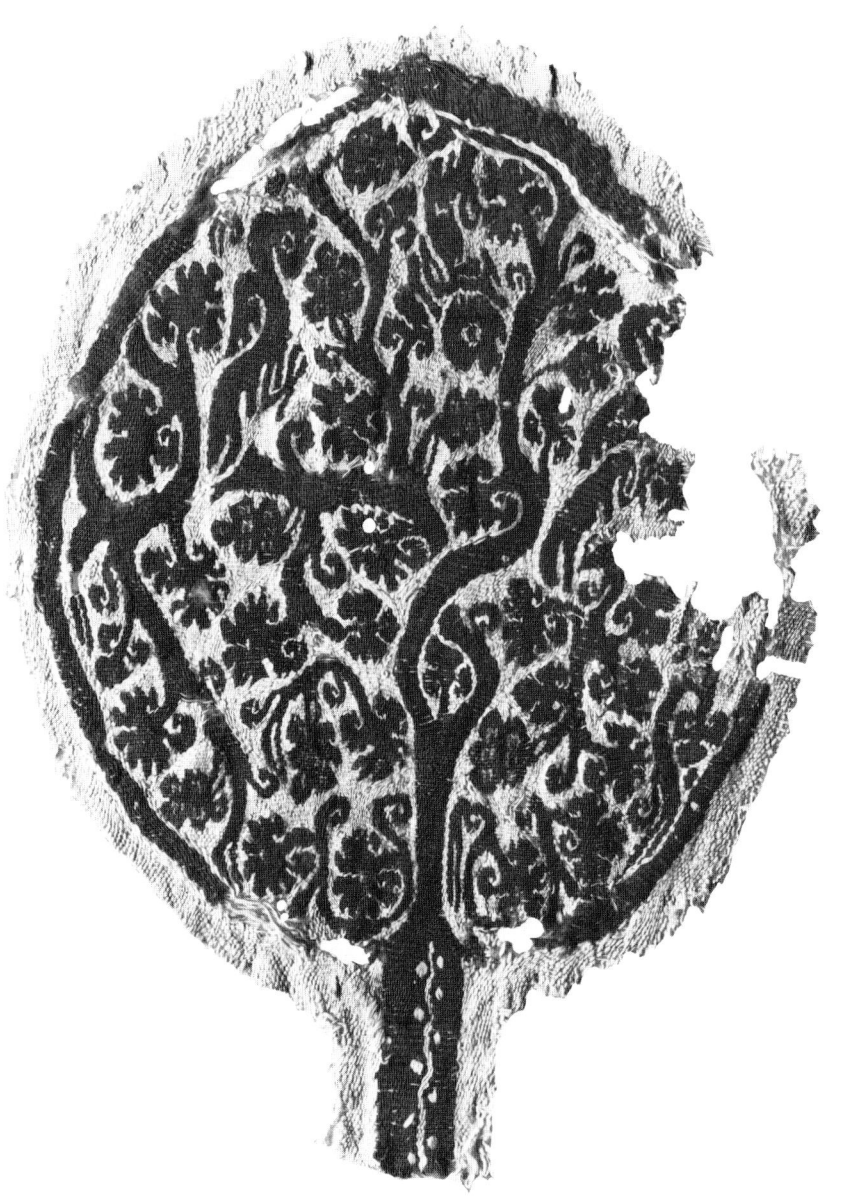

68 Cover or hanging with inhabited vine motifs

Late fourth or early fifth century

The motif of a vine growing from a vase is common in Late Roman tapestries. The vine often encloses birds; sometimes other animals and even human figures are found. For some examples see Toll: *Coptic Textiles*, no. 30, pl. 5; Thompson: *Coptic Textiles in the Brooklyn Museum*, no. 2; Apostolakis: *Ta Koptika Huphasmata*, fig. 83, p. 117; Kybalova: *Coptic Textiles*, fig. 40; Kendrick: *Catalogue of Textiles*, vol. I, nos. 111, 112, 135 and 136, pl. 23; du Bourguet: *Catalogue des étoffes coptes*, nos. C72, C73 and C74; Matie and Liapunova: *Textiles of Coptic Egypt*, pls. 26.2 and 28.1-2. Treatments of this theme vary greatly in complexity; the present example is among the simplest. The drawing, though precise, is rather stiff. The opposite extreme of complexity is represented by cat. no. 67.

The "scale" pattern which decorates the highly stylized leaves at the middle and ends of the band connecting the large roundels is found in a restricted group of textiles. It may therefore be of assistance in establishing the date and affiliations of this tapestry. Examples of the motif include the following: Lewis: *Early Coptic Textiles*, pl. 21; Volbach: *Spätantike und frühmittelalterliche Stoffe*, no. 98, pl. 2; Kendrick: *Catalogue of Textiles*, vol. I, no. 229, pl. 32; du Bourguet: *Catalogue des étoffes coptes*, nos. A13, A14, and C48; Renner: *Die koptischen Stoffe*, pl. 4, no. 5

Tapestry over paired and triple warps in regular alternation, slit and dovetailed; weft wrapping; eccentric wefts; plain weave ground with bands of triple wefts along one edge; plain weave selvedge
Warp: undyed linen
Weft: (tapestry) undyed linen, purple wool, red wool; (plain weave) undyed linen
55½" x 23⅝" (141 cm x 60 cm)
Acquired in 1950 from Phocion Tano, Cairo
71.119

69 Fragment of a curtain or cover with hunting scenes in linked medallions
Fifth century

The pattern of interlaced medallions is probably derived from a conventionalized vine (cf. Shurinova: *Coptic Textiles*, no. 7). In the present example, however, all resemblance to a vine is lost. The animal and plant motifs which fill the medallions link this tapestry to a number of others, none of which are so elaborate; see for example Akashi: *Coptic Textiles*, vol. III, pl. 147, and Apostolakis: *Ta Koptiska Huphasmata*, no. 710, fig. 41.

Tapestry over one warp, slit and dovetailed; weft wrapping; eccentric wefts; plain weave ground with supplementary weft loops
Warp: undyed linen
Weft: (tapestry) undyed linen; undyed, purple, dark blue, green, rust and red wool; (plain weave and loops) undyed linen
44⅞" x 12" (114 cm x 30.5 cm)
Acquired in 1951 from Michel Abemayor, New York
Exhibited: Brooklyn Museum, 1941
Published: *Pagan and Christian Egypt*, Brooklyn, 1941, no. 192
71.121

70 Tunic decoration with animals in interlaced frames
Fifth century

Tapestries with patterns of this type are discussed in von Falke: *Kunstgeschichte der Seidenweberei*, vol. I, pp. 16-20. Surviving examples are numerous; two which closely resemble the present example are Kendrick: *Catalogue of Textiles*, vol. I, no. 80, pl. 26; and du Bourguet: *Catalogue des étoffes coptes*, no. D91.

Tapestry over one warp, slit and dovetailed; weft wrapping; eccentric wefts; sewn to plain weave ground with unwoven area beneath the tapestry
Warp: undyed wool
Weft: (tapestry) undyed linen, purple wool; (plain weave) undyed linen
6¾" x 6¾" (17.6 cm x 17.6 cm) (tapestry only)
Acquired in 1930 from Phocion Tano, Cairo
71.32

71 Tunic decoration with three erotes
Fifth century

The lower border is not continuous with the rest of the piece, but is stylistically identical and must have come from a matching square.

Tapestry over one warp, slit and dovetailed; weft wrapping; eccentric wefts
Warp: undyed wool
Weft: undyed linen, purple wool
6¼" x 5⅞" (16 cm x 15 cm)
Acquired in 1932 from Phocion Tano, Cairo
71.43

72 Tunic decoration with a central bust surrounded by four hares

Fifth century

Four loops enclosing animals are produced by vines springing from vases placed at the midpoints of the four sides of a square. The motif is a fairly common one, and creates an interesting visual rhythm, with emphasis divided between the corners and the sides of the square. A close parallel for the motif, though not for the style of this tapestry, may be found in Apostolakis: *Ta Koptika Huphasmata*, fig. 88, p. 122.

Tapestry over one warp, slit and dovetailed; weft wrapping; eccentric wefts
Warp: undyed wool
Weft: undyed wool, purple wool
9" x 8¼" (23 cm x 21 cm)
Acquired in 1929 from Yamanaka and Co., New York
71.24

73 Tunic decoration with animals in a rincea

Fifth century

For other examples of the style and motif see Toll: *Coptic Textiles*, no. 24, pl. 3; Apostolakis: *Ta Koptika Huphasmata*, fig. 53, p. 90; Peter: *Textilien aus Ägypten*, no. 24; Akashi: *Coptic Textiles*, vol. II, pl. 75; Matie and Liapunova: *Textiles of Coptic Egypt*, pl. 42, nos. 2, 3, 5, 7, 8, 9.

Slit tapestry over one warp; weft wrapping; eccentric wefts
Warp: undyed linen
Weft: undyed linen, dark purple, red and ochre wool
8¼" x 8¼" (21 cm x 21 cm)
Acquired in 1947 from Phocion Tano, Cairo
71.98

74 Tunic with figures and geometric motifs

Sixth century (?)

A comparable tapestry is in the Brooklyn Museum (Thompson: *Coptic Textiles in the Brooklyn Museum*, no. 34).

Tapestry over one warp, slit and dovetailed; weft wrapping; eccentric wefts; plain weave ground; bands of countered extra weft wrapping
Warp: red wool
Weft: (tapestry) black and undyed wool; (plain weave) red wool
48″ x 41½″ (122 cm x 105.5 cm)
Acquired in 1928 from Paul Mallon, Paris
711.8

76 Tunic decoration with fish and human figures

Sixth century (?)

Tapestry over one warp, slit and dovetailed; weft wrapping; eccentric wefts
Warp: undyed wool, pale pink wool
Weft: undyed wool, purple wool
14¾″ x 6⅞″ (37.5 cm x 17.5 cm)
Acquired in 1951 from Phocion Tano, Cairo
71.120

75 Fragment of a *clavus* with dancing figures

Sixth century or later

Compare du Bourguet: *Catalogue des étoffes coptes*, no. H158.

Tapestry over one warp, slit and dovetailed; weft wrapping; eccentric wefts
Warp: tan wool
Weft: undyed wool; blue, red and tan wool
8⅜″ x 4½″ (21.3 cm x 11.5 cm)
Acquired in 1939 from Phocion Tano, Cairo
72.79

77 Fragment of tunic decoration with Pan and a dancing nymph
Sixth century (?)

Tapestry over one warp, slit and dovetailed; weft wrapping; eccentric wefts
Warp: dark blue wool
Weft: undyed wool, dark blue wool
3⅜" x 3¼" (8.5 cm x 8.2 cm)
Acquired in 1942 (provenance unknown)
Exhibited: "Found in Egypt," Textile Museum, 1963
71.81

78 Two fragments of a *clavus* with human and animal figures
Sixth century or later (?)

Slit tapestry over one warp; weft wrapping; eccentric wefts
Warp: undyed linen
Weft: undyed linen, blue wool
6¾" x 3⅜" (17.2 cm x 8.5 cm)
5⅝" x 3½" (14.3 cm x 9 cm)
Acquired in 1930 from Michel Abemayor, New York
711.15

79 Tunic roundel with interlace
First half of the fourth century

The combination of a simple, boldly conceived interlace design with a certain tentativeness in the suggestion of three-dimensionality points to an early date (see Appendix I). Cat. no. 80, while differing in design from this piece, is identical to it in style, size and technique, and is certainly a contemporary product of the same workshop. Other examples of the same approximate style and date in the Museum's collection are cat. nos. 81 and 82.

Slit tapestry over triple warps; weft wrapping; eccentric wefts; plain weave ground
Warp: undyed linen
Weft: (tapestry) undyed linen, purple wool; (plain weave) undyed linen
Diameter of roundel: 7½" (19.1 cm)
Acquired in 1947 from James Pullen, Oakland
Exhibited: "Found in Egypt," Textile Museum, 1963
71.114

80 Tunic roundel with interlace
First half of the fourth century

For general comments see under cat. no. 79.

Slit tapestry over triple warps; weft wrapping; eccentric wefts; plain weave ground
Warp: undyed linen
Weft: (tapestry) undyed linen, purple wool; (plain weave) undyed linen
Diameter of roundel: 7½" (19.1 cm)
Acquired in 1947 from James Pullen, Oakland
Exhibited: "Found in Egypt," Textile Museum, 1963
71.115

81 Border with heads enclosed by interlace
First half of the fourth century

The simplicity of the interlace, and the imprecise drawing, suggest an early date (see Appendix I). The motif occupying the square compartments closely resembles the one contained in the central square of cat. no. 79. For the use of faces in interlace cf. cat. nos. 1 and 83. For a similar interlace strip with alternating squares and roundels, see Errera: *Collection d'anciennes étoffes égyptiennes*, no. 92. Such pieces probably served as borders for curtains.

Tapestry over one warp, slit and dovetailed; weft wrapping; eccentric wefts
Warp: undyed linen
Weft: undyed linen, purple wool
64½" x 5¼" (163.8 cm x 13.4 cm)
Acquired in 1947 from Paul Mallon, Paris
71.92

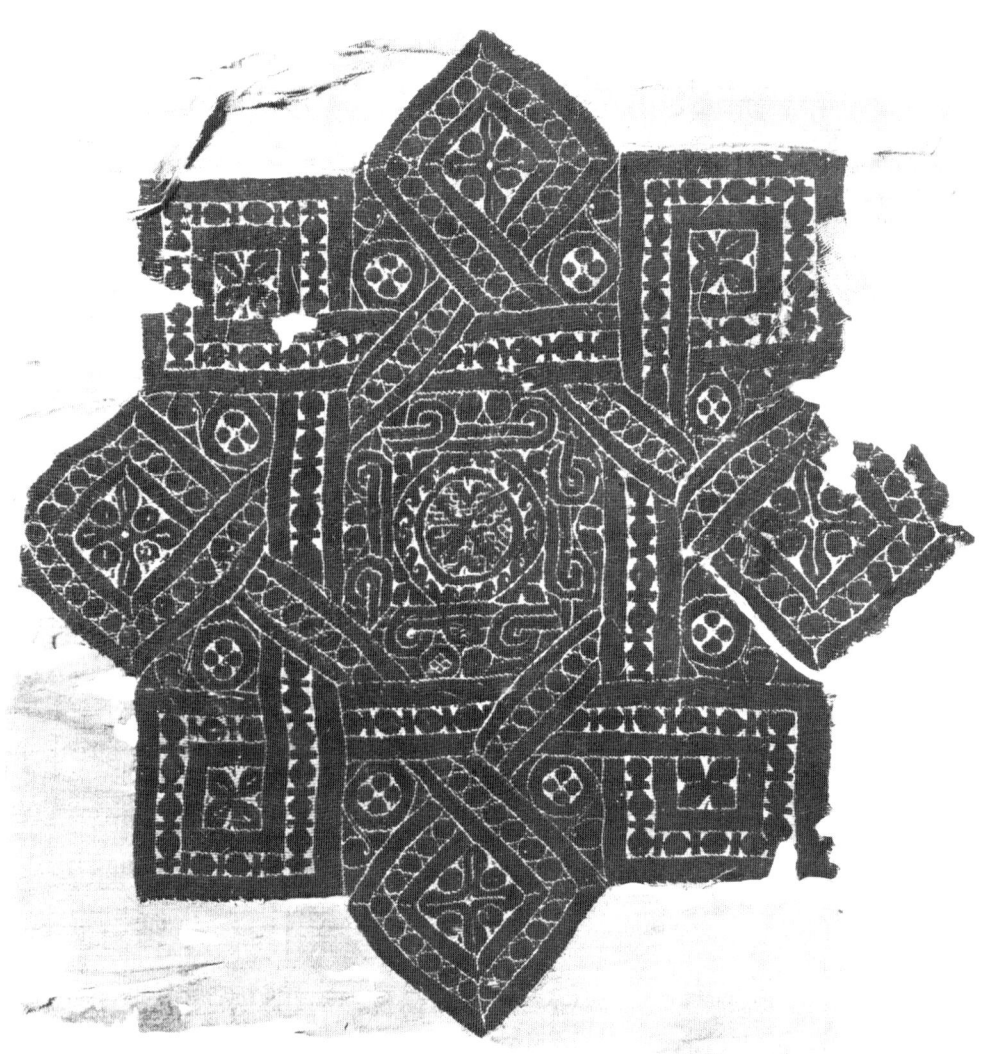

82 Fragment of a curtain (?) with interlace
Middle of the fourth century(?)

As in the preceding pieces, the combination of bold, simple design with imperfect drawing where the bands cross one another points to a fairly early phase of interlace (see Appendix I). However, the use of a secondary interlace motif near the center of the design hints at the elaboration characteristic of the second half of the fourth century. For the origin and evolution of this secondary motif cf. the tapestries cited under cat. no. 97. A tapestry identical to this one in all respects except the central motif is in the Louvre (du Bourguet: *Catalogue des étoffes coptes*, no. All).

Slit tapestry over paired and triple warps in regular alternation; weft wrapping; eccentric wefts; plain weave ground
Warp: undyed linen
Weft: (tapestry) undyed linen, purple wool; (plain weave) undyed linen
19" x 18½" (48.5 cm x 47 cm)
Acquired in 1947 from Phocion Tano, Cairo
71.104

(Color plate 7)

83 Tunic roundel with a human face enclosed by interlace
Mid to late fourth century

Few tapestries woven with gold thread survive, and of these only three bear any stylistic resemblance to this one. Two are in the Abegg-Stiftung Bern in Riggisberg, and one in the Coptic Museum in Cairo (Renner: "Spätantike figürliche Purpurwirkereien," figs. 1–3). It should be noted that the Riggisberg examples are woven on a silk warp, and use gold thread made of gold leaf on a silk core, not linen as here.

This tapestry differs from others of its period in having rather narrow, extremely precisely drawn interlace bands. As a result it seems somewhat static by comparison, but in fact represents a near-perfect balance between intricacy and legibility. The original boldness of the pattern has been greatly diminished by the disappearance of much of the gold leaf. For the dating of the piece see Appendix I.

Slit tapestry over paired warps; weft wrapping; eccentric wefts; plain weave ground with triple wefts at intervals

Warp: undyed linen
Weft: (tapestry) undyed linen, purple wool, gold leaf on linen core; (plain weave) undyed linen
Diameter of roundel: 12½" (31.7 cm)
Acquired in 1947 from Paul Mallon, Paris
Exhibited: "Found in Egypt," Textile Museum, 1963
Published: J. Beckwith: "Coptic Textiles," *Ciba Review*, 12: 133 (Aug. 1959), p. 7 (mention only)
71.91

 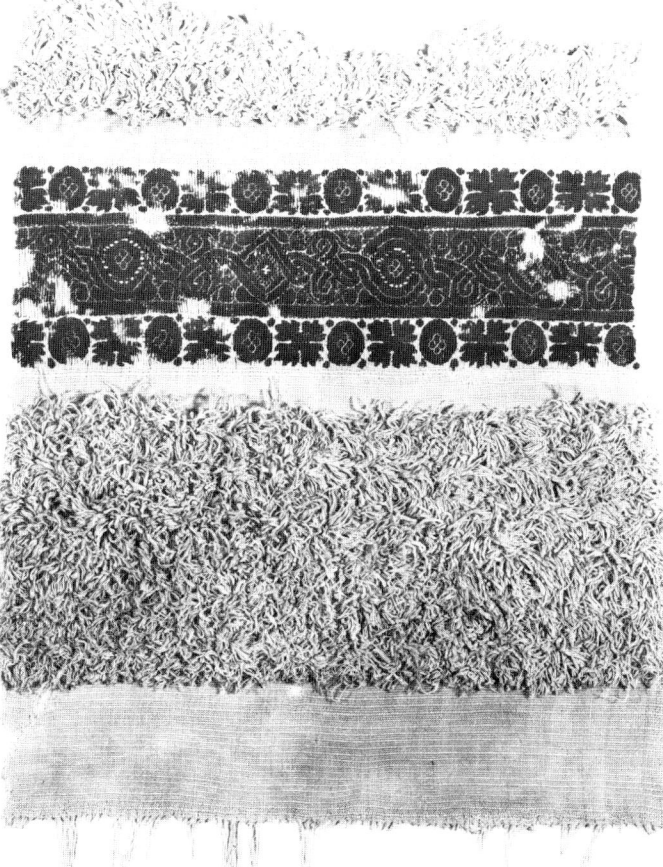

84 Two interlace fragments from a border
Late fourth or early fifth century

Interlace consisting of small, supple loops executed with great freedom and energy is characteristic of the period around the end of fourth century. For further discussion see Appendix I. Small differences in proportion indicate that the two fragments were not originally joined together. However, they are identical in style and were clearly made by a single weaver as part of a set of curtains or furniture covers. The combination of weft-loop pile with tapestry is not uncommon in Late Roman textiles. It may represent a specifically Egyptian tradition, a survival from the Pharaonic period (see Introduction, note 19).

Tapestry over paired and triple warps in regular alternation, slit and dovetailed; weft wrapping; eccentric wefts; plain weave ground with triple wefts at regular intervals and bands of weft-loop pile
Warp: undyed linen
Weft: (tapestry) undyed linen, purple wool; (plain weave and loops) undyed linen
16" x 13½" (40.7 cm x 34.3 cm) (excluding fringe)
14¾" x 13" (37.5 cm x 33 cm) (excluding fringe)
Acquired in 1947 from Phocion Tano, Cairo
71.103

85 Tunic decoration with interlace

First half of the fifth century

The tightness of the loops recalls cat. no. 84, but here they have lost their freedom and liveliness, taking on an almost mechanical appearance. This change, and the breaking down of the pattern into partly or wholly discrete units, argues a later date (see Appendix I).

Tapestry over one warp, slit and dovetailed; weft wrapping; eccentric wefts
Warp: undyed linen
Weft: undyed linen, purple wool, yellow wool
9½" x 9½" (24.1 cm x 24.1 cm)
Acquired in 1947 from James Pullen, Oakland
71.113

86 Fragment with geometric and interlace decoration

Mid-fifth century

The style, the combination of motifs, and the use of a wool warp link this tapestry with cat. nos. 87, 88, 89 and 90. For the dating of the group see Appendix I. A similar textile in Vienna is illustrated in G. Egger: *Koptische Textilien*, pl. 46.

Tapestry over one warp, slit and dovetailed; weft wrapping; eccentric wefts; plain weave ground
Warp: brown wool
Weft: (tapestry) purple, blue, grey-blue, blue-green and undyed wool; undyed linen; plain weave (brown wool)
36½" x 11" (92.7 cm x 28 cm)
Acquired in 1940 from Phocion Tano, Cairo
71.31

87 Roundel from a tunic with geometric, floral and interlace designs
Mid-fifth century

For the stylistic affiliations of this tapestry see cat. no. 86. The dating of the group is discussed in Appendix I. In terms of fineness of weave and delicacy of detail this is probably the finest example of the group in the Museum's collection.

Tapestry over one warp, slit and dovetailed; weft wrapping; eccentric wefts
Warp: undyed wool
Weft: purple wool, undyed linen
Diameter: 8⅜" (21.3 cm)
Acquired in 1933 from Phocion Tano, Cairo
Exhibited: Brooklyn Museum, 1941; "Found in Egypt," Textile Museum, 1963
Published: *Pagan and Christian Egypt*, Brooklyn, 1941, no. 148
71.58

88 Roundel from a tunic with geometric and interlace designs
Mid-fifth century

For the stylistic affiliations of the tapestry see cat. no. 86. The dating of the group is discussed in Appendix I. For an almost identical piece see Akashi: *Coptic Textiles*, vol. I, pl. 38.

Tapestry over one warp, slit and dovetailed; weft wrapping; eccentric wefts
Warp: undyed wool
Weft: undyed wool, purple wool, undyed linen
10¼" x 9¼" (26 cm x 23.5 cm)
Acquired in 1933 from Joseph Brummer, New York
Exhibited: "Found in Egypt," Textile Museum, 1963
71.53

89 Tunic decoration with human figure enclosed by interlace

Mid-fifth century

For the stylistic affiliations of this tapestry see cat. no. 86. The dating of the group is discussed in Appendix I. For a fragment with a human figure virtually identical to the one at the center of this tapestry, see Wulff and Volbach: *Spätantike und Koptische Stoffe*, no. 9632, pl. 63.

Tapestry over one warp, slit and dovetailed; weft wrapping; eccentric wefts; sewn to a plain weave ground
Warp: undyed wool
Weft: purple wool, undyed wool, undyed linen
Plain weave: undyed linen
6¼" x 7" (17.2 cm x 17.8 cm) (tapestry only)
Acquired in 1947 from Phocion Tano, Cairo
71.96

90 Napkin (?) with animal figures enclosed by interlace

Mid-fifth century(?)

For the stylistic affiliations of the tapestry see cat. no. 86. Although the animal motif is unusual if not unique in a frame of this type, the tapestry is probably to be included in the same group as the works just mentioned. The dating of the group is discussed in Appendix I.

For a textile of similar overall design cf. Kendrick: *Catalogue of Textiles*, vol. II, no. 323, pl. 9.

Plain weave with tapestry over one warp, slit and dovetailed; weft wrapping; eccentric wefts
Warp: undyed wool
Weft: (tapestry) undyed wool, purple wool, undyed linen; (plain weave) undyed wool, red wool
23¼" x 15¼" (59 cm x 38.7 cm) (excluding fringe)
Acquired in 1947 from James Pullen, Oakland
71.105

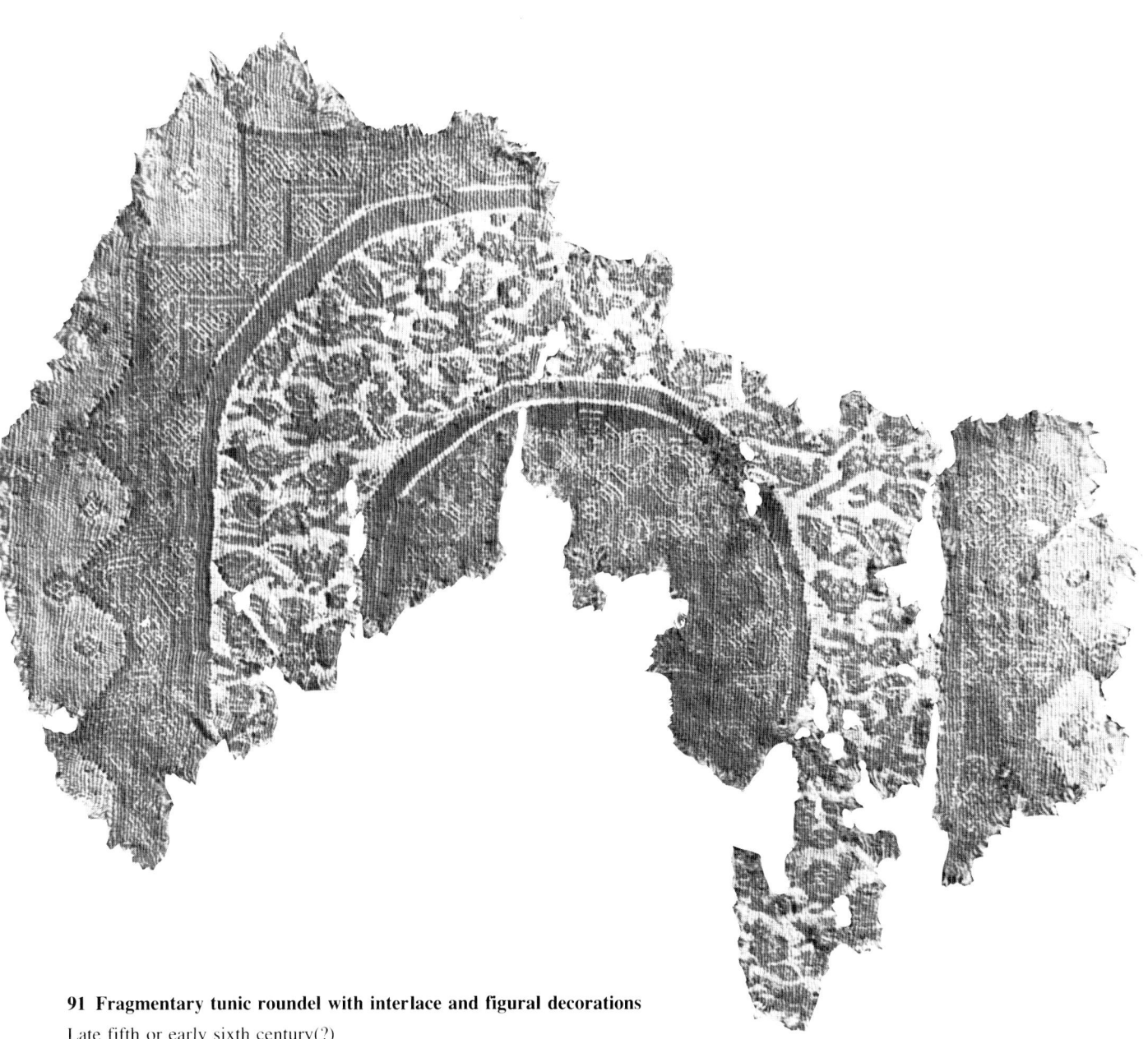

91 Fragmentary tunic roundel with interlace and figural decorations

Late fifth or early sixth century(?)

The style of the interlace falls between that of the mid-fifth century, represented by cat. nos. 87–90, and that of the sixth, represented by cat. nos. 92–95. The implications of this style and the dating of the piece are discussed in Appendix I. For decoration consisting of a scattering of highly simplified and distorted human and animal figures, cf. Baginski and Tidhar: *Textiles from Egypt*, nos. 237 and 238; du Bourguet: *Catalogue des étoffes coptes*, no. 112; and Peter: *Textilien aus Ägypten*, no. 53.

Tapestry over one warp, slit and dovetailed; weft wrapping; eccentric wefts
Warp: rust-colored wool
Weft: red, rust-colored and undyed wool
Maximum dimension: 12½" (31.8 cm)
Acquired in 1947 from Phocion Tano, Cairo
71.94

92 Tunic decoration with interlace designs and human and animal figures
Sixth century

This is one of a large group of closely related tapestries, which is further represented in the Museum's collection by cat. nos. 94 and 95, and at somewhat greater remove by cat. nos. 93 and 96. For the dating of these works see Appendix I. The group is characterized by an elaborate but stiff—almost mechanical—interlace style, and often by the inclusion of human figures that are crude to the point of infantilism. Typically, one or two fingers on each hand are transformed into elongated hooks.

For other textiles of this type see the following: Baginski and Tidhar: *Textiles from Egypt*, nos. 252, 254 and 256; Billeter: *Aussereuropäische Textilien*, nos. 11-198 and 1961-55; du Bourguet: *Catalogue des étoffes coptes*, nos. 123, 129, 134, 136, 137, etc.; Shurinova: *Coptic Textiles*, no. 169.

Tapestry over one warp, slit and dovetailed; weft wrapping; eccentric wefts; plain weave ground
Warp: undyed wool
Weft: (tapestry) undyed, dark blue (?), red and green wool; (plain weave) undyed wool
17" x 9¾" (43.2 cm x 24.8 cm)
Acquired in 1938 from Phocion Tano, Cairo
72.72

93 Tunic decoration with interlace
Sixth century

For the date and affiliations of this tapestry see under cat. no. 92. An almost identical piece is in the Kelsey Museum of Archaeology, University of Michigan (Wilson: *Ancient Textiles from Egypt*, no. 146, pl. 13).

Slit tapestry over one warp; weft wrapping; eccentric wefts; plain weave ground with bands of countered extra-weft wrapping
Warp: undyed wool
Weft: (tapestry) undyed wool, purple wool, undyed linen; (plain weave) undyed wool
29¼" x 9¼" (74.3 cm x 23.5 cm)
Acquired in 1940 from Phocion Tano, Cairo
711.18

94 Fragment with interlace and human figures
Sixth century

For the date and affiliations of this tapestry see under cat. no. 92. Cf. also du Bourguet: *Catalogue des étoffes coptes,* nos. 158, 160, 163, etc.

Tapestry over one warp, slit and dovetailed; weft wrapping; eccentric wefts; plain weave ground
Warp: tan wool
Weft: (tapestry) undyed, tan, purple, red and green wool; undyed linen; (plain weave) purple wool, tan wool
13½" x 7" (34.3 cm x 17.8 cm) (excluding fringe)
Acquired in 1964 from Royal Athena Galleries, New York
1964.17.1

95 Tunic decoration with interlace and figures
Sixth century

For the date and affiliations of this tapestry see under cat. no. 92.

Tapestry over one warp, slit and dovetailed; weft wrapping; eccentric wefts; plain weave ground with bands of countered extra-weft wrapping
Warp: undyed wool
Weft: (tapestry) undyed wool, purple wool, traces of linen; (plain weave) undyed wool
Acquired in 1948 from James Pullen, Oakland
Extreme dimensions: 8¾" x 8" (22.2 cm x 20.3 cm)
72.151

96 Tunic fragment (shoulder square and *clavus*) with interlace and human figures
Late sixth century(?)

The stiffness of the interlace, and the reduction of the greater part of it to a series of simple loops, places this work near the end of the long history of interlace-patterned tapestries. For the dating and affiliations of the piece see under cat. no. 92. For almost identical fragments see du Bourguet: *Catalogue des étoffes coptes*, nos. 184 and 191; Billeter: *Aussereuropäische Textilien*, no. 1958-240.

Tapestry over one warp, slit and dovetailed; weft wrapping; eccentric wefts; plain weave ground with bands of countered extra-weft wrapping
Warp: undyed wool
Weft: (tapestry) undyed, purple, red and green wool, undyed linen; (plain weave) undyed wool
Extreme dimensions: 26¼" x 15⅜" (66.7 cm x 39 cm)
Acquired in 1932 from Phocion Tano, Cairo
Exhibited: Brooklyn Museum, 1941; Rhode Island School of Design Museum of Art, 1947; Essen, Villa Hügel, 1963; Paris, Petit Palais, 1964
Published: *Pagan and Christian Egypt*, Brooklyn, 1941, no. 151; *Koptische kunst*, Essen-Bredeney, 1963, no. 307; *l'Art copte*, Paris, 1964, no. 216
72.35

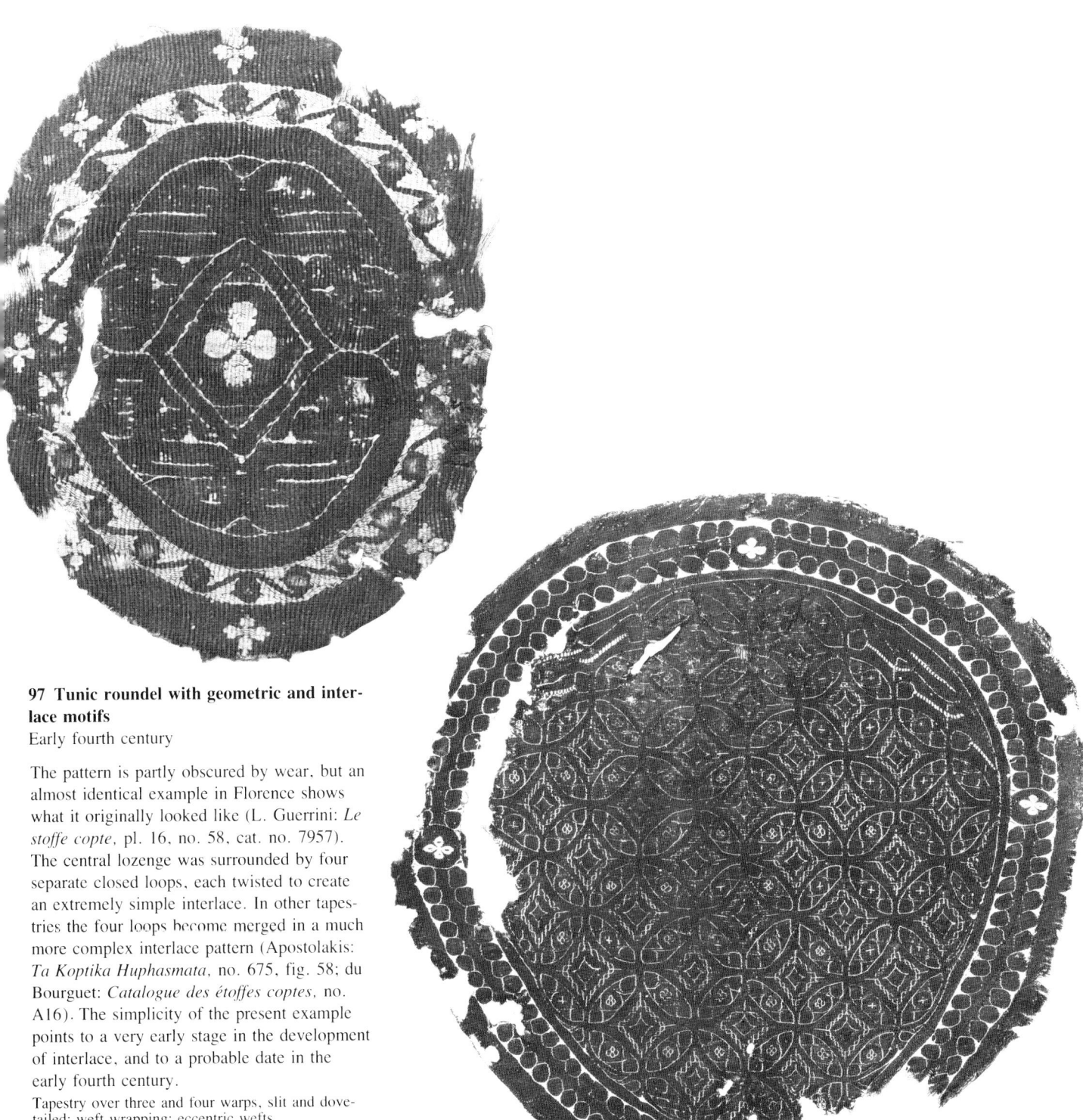

97 Tunic roundel with geometric and interlace motifs
Early fourth century

The pattern is partly obscured by wear, but an almost identical example in Florence shows what it originally looked like (L. Guerrini: *Le stoffe copte*, pl. 16, no. 58, cat. no. 7957). The central lozenge was surrounded by four separate closed loops, each twisted to create an extremely simple interlace. In other tapestries the four loops become merged in a much more complex interlace pattern (Apostolakis: *Ta Koptika Huphasmata*, no. 675, fig. 58; du Bourguet: *Catalogue des étoffes coptes*, no. A16). The simplicity of the present example points to a very early stage in the development of interlace, and to a probable date in the early fourth century.

Tapestry over three and four warps, slit and dovetailed; weft wrapping; eccentric wefts
Warp: undyed linen
Weft: undyed linen, blue wool
8" x 6¼" (20.3 cm x 15.9 cm)
Acquired in 1947 from Phocion Tano, Cairo
71.97

98 Roundel with geometric design
Fourth century

For the development of the motif see Appendix I, especially note 8. Compare also Kendrick: *Catalogue of Textiles*, vol. I, no. 199, pl. 29; Akashi: *Coptic Textiles*, vol. III, pl. 141a; Egger: *Koptische Textilien*, pl. 3.

Tapestry over one warp, slit and dovetailed; weft wrapping; eccentric wefts
Warp: undyed linen
Weft: undyed linen, purple wool
Diameter of roundel: 18½" (47 cm)
Acquired in 1931 from Paul Mallon, Paris
71.34

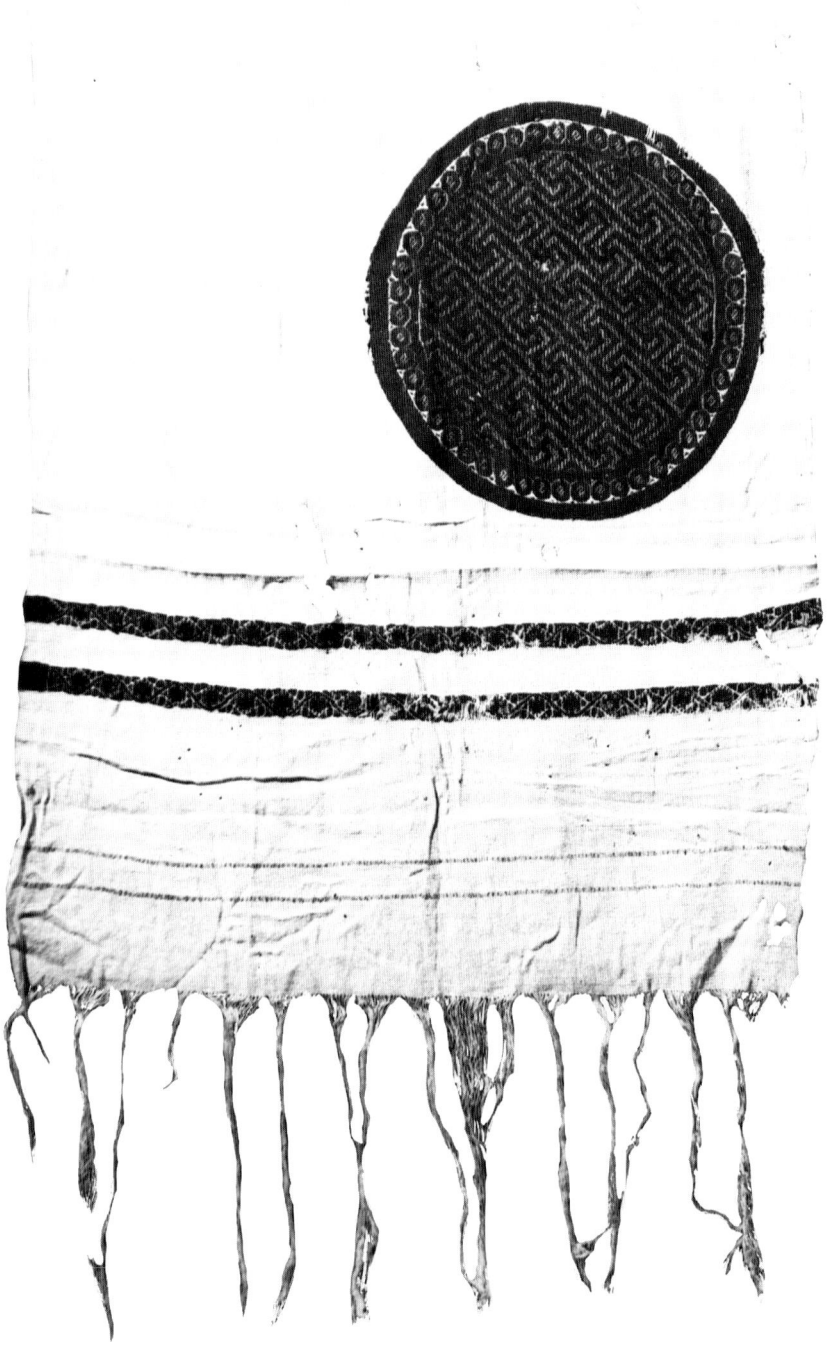

99 Fragment of a shroud(?)
Fourth or fifth century

The conclusion that this fragment is part of a shroud is based on its resemblance to a textile illustrated in Errera: *Collection d'anciennes étoffes égyptiennes*, no. 85. For the use of such shrouds see Guimet: *Les portraits d'Antinoë*, figs. 72 and 75.

The problem of dating pieces whose primary motif is the meander is discussed under cat. no. 100. Unfortunately in the present case the lack of other evidence permits only the most general dating. For other examples of the motif see Shurinova: *Coptic Textiles*, nos. 31, 32 and 107; du Bourguet: *Catalogue des étoffes coptes*, no. A23; Akashi: *Coptic Textiles*, vol. III, pl. 120; Kendrick: *Catalogue of Textiles*, vol. I, no. 193, pl. 28; E. Errera: *Collection d'anciennes étoffes égyptiennes*, no. 68; Guerrini: *Le stoffe copte*, cat. no. 9703, pl. 9.

Tapestry over paired and triple warps in regular alternation, slit and dovetailed (?); weft wrapping; eccentric wefts; plain weave ground
Warp: undyed linen
Weft: (tapestry) undyed linen, purple wool; (plain weave) undyed linen
28¾" x 23½" (73 cm x 59.7 cm) (excluding fringe); diameter of roundel: 11⅞" (30.2 cm)
Acquired in 1948 from James Pullen, Oakland
72.153

100 Tunic decoration with meanders
First half of the fifth century(?)

The meander, also known as the fret or key pattern, is very common in Late Roman art (cf. cat. no. 99), and its popularity and resistance to change make it difficult to date individual examples without the evidence of other motifs. In this case the telling theme is the square with three leaves growing from opposite sides. In one example a square of this type, actually containing a meander, is associated with the angular interlace that is characteristic of the first half of the fifth century (D. Renner: *Die koptischen Stoffe*, cat. no. 5, pl. 4; for the dating of the interlace see Appendix I). In another, the square contains interlace of this type (Shurinova: *Coptic Textiles*, no. 22). These comparisons suggest a date in the first half of the fifth century, but such a dating should be regarded only as tentative, since the total lifespan of the motif has not been determined. Of the other published examples, those closest to this one are Kendrick: *Catalogue of Textiles*, vol. I, no. 209, pl. 4, and Wulff and Volbach: *Spätantike und koptische Stoffe*, no. 9119, pl. 78.

Tapestry over paired and triple warps in regular alternation, slit and dovetailed; weft wrapping; eccentric wefts; plain weave ground
Warp: undyed linen
Weft: (tapestry) undyed linen, purple wool; (plain weave) undyed linen
Maximum dimensions of pattern: 10" x 5⅝" (25.4 cm x 14.3 cm)
Acquired in 1952 from Joseph Costa, New York
71.126

101 Tunic decoration with interlace

Early fifth century(?)

The outline of the pattern—a roundel developing into diametrically opposed knotlike interlace projections—is found in two tapestries which also contain interlace typical of the first half of the fifth century (Egger: *Koptische Textilien*, pl. 1; Kybalova: *Coptic Textiles*, no. 74, p. 123; for the dating of these pieces by their interlace style see Appendix 1). The central interlace of this tapestry lacks both the angularity and the extreme elaboration of the works just cited, suggesting a somewhat earlier date. However, it clearly displays the fragmentation of pattern which is characteristic of early fifth-century tapestries. A date shortly after 400 therefore seems likely.

Tapestry over paired and triple warps in regular alternation, slit and dovetailed; weft wrapping; eccentric wefts; plain weave ground

Warp: undyed linen

Weft: (tapestry) undyed linen, purple wool; (plain weave) undyed linen

Extreme dimensions of pattern: 13⅞" x 8¼" (35.3 cm x 21 cm)

Acquired in 1947 from Phocion Tano, Cairo
71.99

102 Roundel from a tunic

Fifth century

Tapestry over one warp, slit and dovetailed; weft wrapping; eccentric wefts

Warp: red wool

Weft: purple, brown, and undyed wool; undyed linen

Diameter: 8⅝" (22 cm)

Acquired in 1932 from Phocion Tano, Cairo

Exhibited: American Federation of Arts Loan Exhibition, 1935-36; "Found in Egypt," Textile Museum, 1963; "Myth and Gospel: Art of Coptic Egypt," Newark Museum, 1977-78

Published: Riefstahl, Catalogue of A.F.A. Loan Exhibition, p. 5, no. 2
71.42

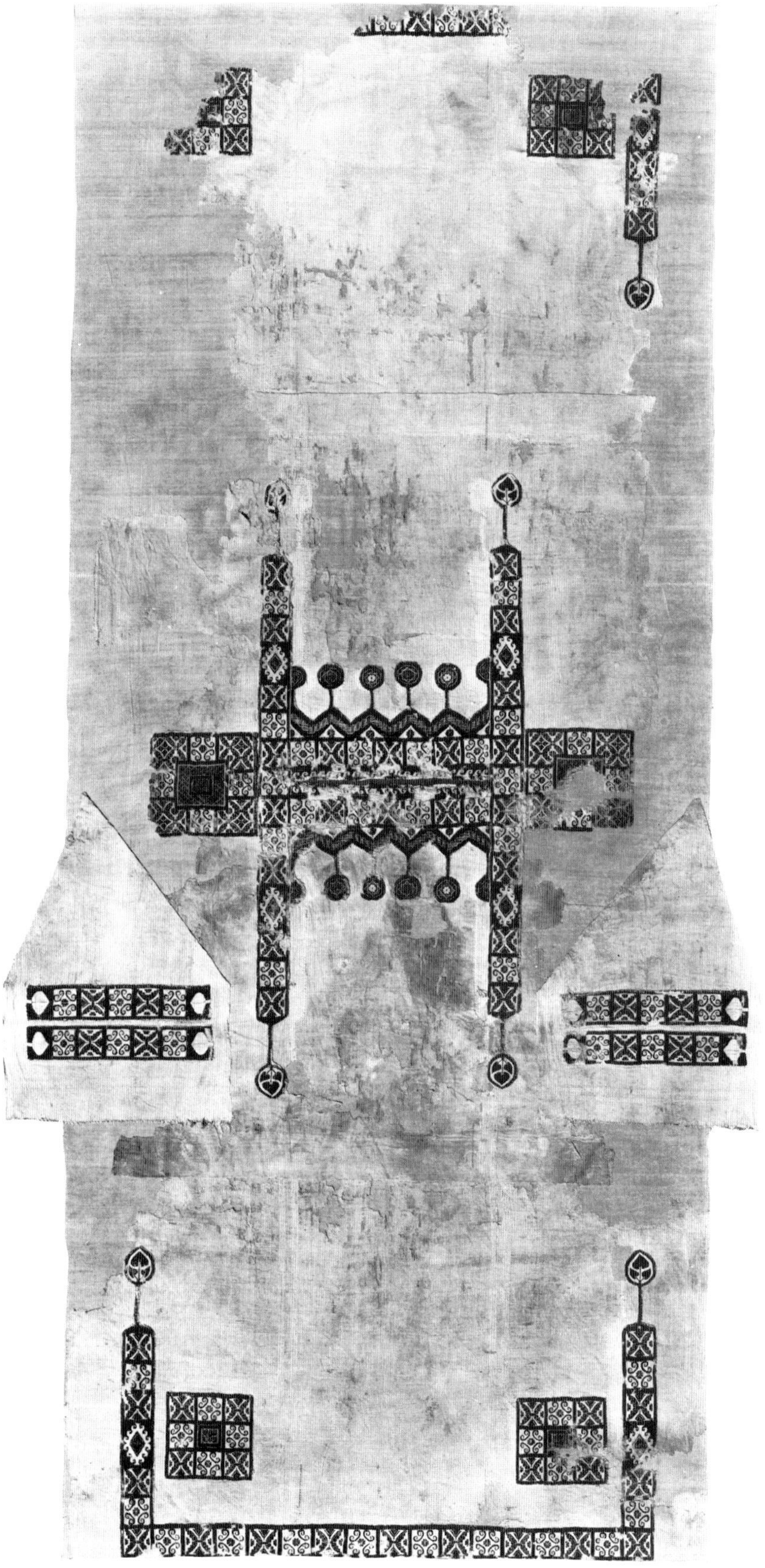

103 Tunic with floral and geometric decoration
Sixth century

For similar geometric motifs see du Bourguet: *Catalogue des étoffes coptes*, no. H97.
Slit tapestry over paired warps; weft wrapping; eccentric wefts; sewn to plain weave ground with triple wefts at regular intervals
Warp: undyed linen
Weft: (tapestry) undyed linen, purple wool; (plain weave) undyed linen
86½" x 43½" (219.7 cm x 110.5 cm)
Acquired in 1932 from Phocion Tano, Cairo
71.48

TEXTILES WITH PATTERNS IN WEFT-LOOP PILE

In addition to tapestries, Late Antique weavers also produced a number of textiles with patterns of supplementary-weft loops standing out from a plain-weave ground. (On this technique see Emery: *The Primary Structures of Fabrics*, p. 148.) This method of weaving is less precise than tapestry, but is capable of subtle color gradations and impressionistic effects. (See for example *Pagan and Christian Egypt*, no. 183; Kybalova: *Coptic Textiles*, no. 6, p. 57; and Wessel: *Coptic Art*, fig. 105, p. 180.) The same technique can also be used to create bold, unmodulated forms, both geometric and figural. The four examples illustrated here belong to this second category. In the case of figural textiles it is generally assumed that the simple style is later than the impressionistic one. However, as with tapestries, one should remember that classical and folk traditions often coexisted.

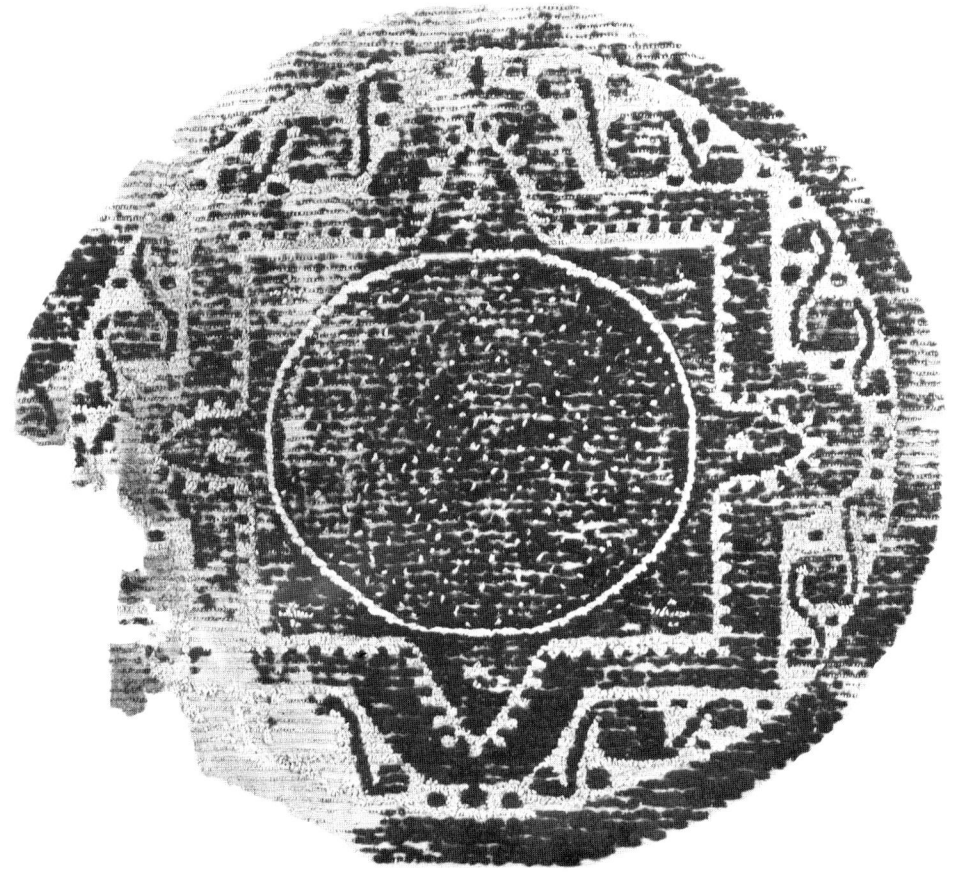

104 Roundel with a geometric design
Fourth or fifth century

An identical roundel is in the Victoria and Albert Museum (Kendrick: *Catalogue of Textiles*, vol. I, no. 8, pl. 3); cf. also Errera: *Collection d'anciennes étoffes égyptiennes*, no. 78, and du Bourguet: *Catalogue des étoffes coptes*, no. D31.

Plain weave with supplementary wefts and weft loops
Warp: undyed linen
Weft: undyed linen
Loops: undyed linen, purple wool
21" x 18⅞" (53.5 cm x 48 cm)
Acquired in 1932 from Phocion Tano, Cairo
Exhibited: Rhode Island School of Design Museum, 1947; "Found in Egypt," Textile Museum, 1963
71.45

105 Octagon with a geometric design
Fourth or fifth century

The same motif appears in a looped textile in the Victoria and Albert Museum (Kendrick: *Catalogue of Textiles,* vol. I, no. 36, pl. 11).
Plain weave with supplementary wefts and weft loops
Warp: undyed linen
Weft: undyed linen
Loops: undyed linen; undyed, purple, red, pink, orange, yellow and green wool
16½" x 14½" (42 cm x 37 cm)
Acquired in 1947 from Phocion Tano, Cairo
71.112

106 Fragment of a hanging with a standing figure and a candlestick
Fifth or sixth century

Similar textiles are discussed by G. de Francovich in "L'Egitto, la Siria e Costantinopoli: problemi di metodo" (*Rivista dell' Istituto Nazionale d'Archeologia e Storia dell'Arte,* n.s. 11-12 (1963), pp. 83-229) pp. 151ff. See also D. Shepherd, "Saints and a 'Sinner' on Two Coptic Textiles," *Bulletin of the Cleveland Museum of Art,* November 1974, pp. 331-338. The fragmentary inscription reads ΛΑ (LA).

Plain weave with supplementary weft loops. (The ground has been pieced with fragments of plain weave not originally belonging to this textile.)
Warp: undyed linen
Weft: undyed linen
Loops: undyed linen; undyed, light and dark blue, rose, pink and beige wool
16⅛" x 13⅜" (41 cm x 34 cm)
Acquired in 1932 from Max von Oppenheim, New York
Exhibited: Brooklyn Museum, 1941; Rhode Island School of Design Museum, 1947; Andover, Addison Gallery (Phillips Academy), 1947; American Federation of Arts, "Abstract Art in Ancient Textiles," 1959-60; Essen, Villa Hügel, 1963; Zürich, Kunsthaus, 1963-64; Vienna, Akademie der bildenden Künste, 1964; Paris, Petit Palais, 1964
Published: *Pagan and Christian Egypt,* Brooklyn, 1941, cat. no. 249; *Koptische Kunst,* Essen-Bredeney, 1963, cat. no. 280, illus.; *Koptische Kunst,* Zürich, 1963, cat. no. 251; *Frühchristliche und koptische Kunst,* Vienna, 1964, cat. no. 133, illus.; *L'Art copte,* Paris, 1964, cat. no. 173; W.F. Volbach: *Early Decorative Textiles,* London and New York, 1969, pl. 33
71.46

107 Fragment of a curtain or hanging with a lion and an eagle
Sixth century or later

Closely related fragments are preserved in the Abegg-Stiftung Bern in Riggisberg and in the Ikonenmuseum, Recklinghausen (D. Shepherd, "Saints and a 'Sinner' on Two Coptic Textiles," *Bulletin of the Cleveland Museum of Art,* November, 1974, pp. 331-338, figs. 2 and 8).

Plain weave with supplementary wefts and weft loops
Warp: undyed linen
Weft: undyed linen
Loops: undyed linen, red, green, blue, brown and ochre wool;
42⅝" x 35¼" (108.4 cm x 65.5 cm)
Acquired in 1960 from Christian Grand, Zürich
Exhibited: "Found in Egypt," Textile Museum, 1963; "Treasures from the Museum's Collections," Textile Museum, 1971
1960.5.1

DRAWLOOM TEXTILES IN WOOL AND SILK

All the textiles illustrated so far are woven in the tapestry technique. Another method of pattern weaving was also in use in Late Antiquity, namely weaving on a drawloom. The origin, design and capabilities of the Late Antique drawloom have long been a subject of discussion, not to say controversy.[1] However, the fundamental difference between the two methods is not in doubt. Unlike the tapestry loom, the drawloom allows the warps to be raised and lowered mechanically and in a predetermined sequence. This vastly facilitates the production of complex repeated patterns.

The drawloom is best known for the great achievements in silk weaving that it made possible, but in a less complex form it was also used in weaving wool. A number of early drawloom wool fabrics have been preserved.[2] They are generally dated in the fifth century, and some at least must represent the earliest phase of drawloom weaving.[3] What almost all of them have in common is a tentativeness or awkwardness of design which suggests that the weavers had not yet adjusted to the problem of creating patterns based on the repetition of a limited number of elements. There is evidence that drawloom weaving, at least in wool, began as a labor-saving technique. A fifth-century textile in the Victoria and Albert Museum combines drawloom weaving with areas of tapestry.[4] As Louisa Bellinger has pointed out, "The tapestry pattern is much finer and more delicate than the drawloom pattern and seems to show that the latter was a faster but, at least at first, a less particular method of decoration."[5] If this is the case it is possible that drawloom weaving in wool was never a "high" art, and that weavers using this method lacked the incentive or the skill to create imaginative and harmonious patterns.

Silk weaving, an important facet of Early Byzantine art, exhibits none of the tentativeness that characterizes the woolen fabrics. While naturally subject to variation in quality, it never suggests an inability to solve the problems of design posed by the medium and technique. Two very different approaches to design dominate Early Byzantine silk weaving. Both probably emerged around the beginning of the sixth century. In the first, a number of small decorative elements, abstract and figural, are arranged close together, either in registers or in a grid.[6] The effect is delicate, some-

---

1. See for example the following works, which discuss the drawloom in its relation to Late Antique textiles: J.F. Flanagan, "The Origin of the Drawloom Used in the Making of Early Byzantine Silks," *The Burlington Magazine*, 35 (1919), pp. 167-172; G.M. Crowfoot and J. Griffiths, "Coptic Textiles in Two-Faced Weave with Pattern in Reverse," *Journal of Egyptian Archaeology*, 25 (1939), pp. 40-47; R. Pfister, "Le rôle de l'Iran dans les textiles d'Antinoë," *Ars Islamica*, 13-14 (1948), pp. 46-74; L. Bellinger, "Textile Analysis: Early Techniques in Egypt and the Near East" (pt. 3), *Textile Museum Workshop Notes*, Paper no. 6, November, 1952. Much of the literature on the subject concerns the question of whether the technique of drawloom weaving was borrowed from Persia. This question is bound up with that of the Persian origin of a number of Late Antique textiles and textile motifs; see below, note 6.

2. For some of the most important drawloom wool fabrics see the following: Kendrick: *Catalogue of Textiles*, vol. II, no. 537, pl. 35; C.J. Lamm and R.J. Charleston, "Some Early Egyptian Drawloom Weavings," *Bulletin de la Société d'Archéologie Copte*, 5 (1939); M.S. Dimand, "Early Christian Weavings from Egypt," *Bulletin of the Metropolitan Museum of Art*, 20 (1925), pp. 55-58, figs. 1 and 3; Dimand, "Coptic and Egypto-Arabic Textiles," *Bulletin of the Metropolitan Museum of Art*, 26 (1939), pp. 89-91, fig. 1; *Pagan and Christian Egypt*, no. 181; Pfister, *op. cit.* (note 1), fig. 60; Weibel: *Two Thousand Years of Textiles*, no. 38.

3. Flanagan, *op. cit.* (note 1); Bellinger, *op. cit.* (note 1).

4. Kendrick: *Catalogue of Textiles*, vol. II, no. 537, pl. 25.

5. Bellinger, *op. cit.* (note 1).

6. Silks of this type are closely associated with Antinoë in Egypt, where most of them were discovered around the turn of the century. Unfortunately the Antinoë silks were dispersed immediately after their discovery, and no record was kept of the contexts in which they were found. The literature on the silks is extensive, and centers for the most part on problems of dating and on the question of whether they were woven in the Mediterranean world or in Persia. Some of the most important studies of the Antinoë silks

times whimsical, often elegant. Three silks in the Textile Museum's collection, cat. nos. 112, 113 and 114, belong to this large category. The other type of pattern consists of a series of uniform tangent or interlaced circular medallions containing animals or human figures. The size of these medallions varies from textile to textile; in some cases they are a few inches in diameter, in others as much as a yard.[7] Where the grid patterns are gaily sumptuous, the medallion silks can be imposing, even monumental. Although the Museum possesses no Byzantine textiles of such size or power, cat. no. 115 reflects the same tradition on a smaller scale and in a less grandiose style.

The following structural analysis of the textiles in this section has been prepared by Ann Pollard Rowe, Curator of Western Hemisphere Textiles at the Textile Museum. I take this opportunity to express my gratitude for her help.

WOOL TEXTILES

All are complementary-weft weave, with 3-span floats in alternate alignment (3/1 order of interlacing). See Irene Emery, *The Primary Structures of Fabrics*, pp. 150-151, figs. 246-249. The warps are alternately single and paired. It is the "inner" warps that are paired. There are 2/2 vertical color changes (see Ann Pollard Rowe, *Warp-Patterned Weaves of the Andes*, Washington, 1977, p. 67). In two of the pieces (cat. nos. 110 and 111) one of the sets of wefts has discontinuous elements with a vertical join. In cat. no. 110, this is produced with double interlocking. Cat. no. 111 is probably the same but this cannot be verified since the piece is mounted without a window. Two of the pieces (cat nos. 108 and 109) have bands of weft-faced plain weave, interlacing 3/3.

Two of the pieces have pile on the back. The pile differs in each case. In cat. no. 109 the pile is formed by extra weft slip loops, with the loops drawn under two warps.

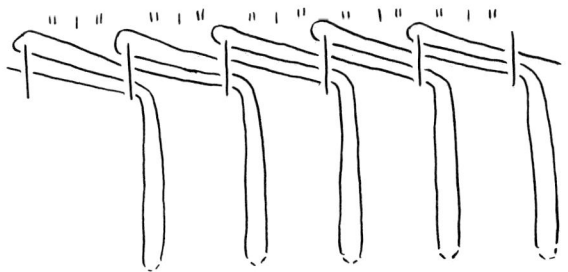

This terminology is explained and a simpler version of the structure illustrated in Emery (*op. cit.*), pp. 223-224, fig. 348. The warps used to secure the pile are alternate singles. In cat. no. 110, the pile does not appear to be slip loops because the two ends that twist together do not come out in the same place.

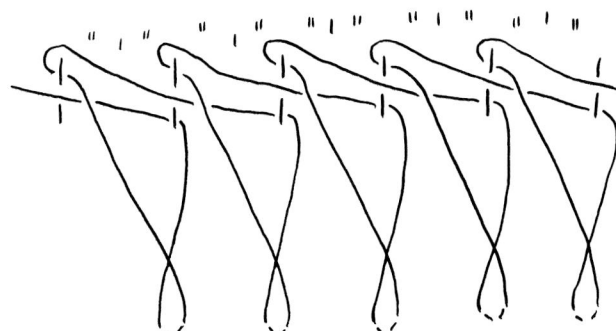

Instead, the pile is formed by overlapping Sehna "knots" (a form of extra-weft wrapping), using alternate single warps.

SILK TEXTILES

All are complementary-weft weave with 5-span floats in diagonal alignment (5/1 order of interlacing, diagonal developed on alternate warps). See Emery (*op. cit.*) p. 153, figs. 256-257. One of the silks has a third color appearing in horizontal bands, so that in these areas, the two unused colors are paired on the back. One of the silks is woven in four colors, with the three unused colors carried parallel to each other on the back. All the wefts seem to be continuous.

---

are these: O. von Falke: *Kunstgeschichte der Seidenweberei*, vol. I, pp. 31-38; R. Pfister, "La decoration des étoffes d'Antinoë," *Revue des Arts Asiatiques*, 5 (1928), pp. 215-243; E. Kitzinger, "The Horse and Lion Tapestry at Dumbarton Oaks," *Dumbarton Oaks Papers*, 3 (1946), pp. 1-72; Pfister, *op. cit.* (note 1); A. Geijer, "A Silk from Antinoë and the Sassanian Textile Art," *Orientalia Suecana*, 12 (1963), pp. 3-36. Pfister is the strongest advocate of an early date and a Persian origin; his views are summarized and defended in Geijer's article. Kitzinger, while agreeing that the silks show a considerable amount of Persian influence, argues that they were woven in Egypt around the beginning of the sixth century.

7. See for example the silks illustrated in H. Pierce and R. Tyler, "The Prague Rider-Silk and the Persian-Byzantine Problem," *The Burlington Magazine*, 68 (1936), pp. 213-220.

(Color plate 8)

108 Cover with geometric designs
Fifth century

The variety and elaborateness of its design make this textile unique among early drawloom wool fabrics. The various patterns of interlocking polygons are more typical of floor mosaics than of textiles, but are occasionally found in Late Antique tapestries (cf. Errera: *Collection d'anciennes étoffes égyptiennes*, no. 55; Guerrini: *Le stoffe copte,* no. 29, cat. no. 7999, pl. 7). A similar pattern appears in an early "drawloom" fabric which may in fact have been woven on a four-harness loom (Crowfoot and Griffiths, "Coptic Textiles in Two-Faced Weave," no. 1). For a phase intermediate in complexity between this and the Textile Museum's example, cf. du Bourguet: *Catalogue des étoffes coptes*, no. I20. Some of the jagged motifs which separate the wider bands of ornament have parallels in other textiles: cf. du Bourguet, nos. D12 (tapestry), G3 (drawloom), and I21 (drawloom). The wide bands of highly stylized zigzagging vines may be a more elaborate version of a motif found in several tapestries; cf. Toll: *Coptic Textiles,* nos. 10 and 14, pl. 2, and Metropolitan Museum of Art, no. 89.18.62. Other drawloom fabrics furnish no parallel to the masks which decorate two of the sets of polygons, but there may be a connection with crude tapestry masks; cf. Kendrick: *Catalogue of Textiles,* vol. II, no. 328, pl. 10.

Complementary-weft weave with three-span floats in alternating alignment with 2/2 vertical color changes; plain bands in weft-faced plain weave interlacing 3/3; alternating single and paired warps
Warp: undyed wool
Weft: red, yellow, blue-green and navy blue wool
93¼" x 59⅜" (239 cm x 129 cm)
Acquired in 1950 from Phocion Tano, Cairo
31.11

109 Cover with a design of human and animal figures
Fifth century

For the closest parallel to this textile cf. Dimand, "Coptic and Egypto-Arabic Textiles," fig. 1.

Complementary-weft weave with three-span floats in alternating alignment with 2/2 vertical color changes; alternating single and paired warps
Warp: undyed wool
Weft: undyed wool, red wool
Pile: red wool
94" x 52¼" (238.6 cm x 132.7 cm)
Provenance and date of acquisition unknown

110 Cover with a pattern of lions
Fifth century

In addition to the textiles cited in the introduction to this section (note 2), see R. Jaques and E. Flemming: *Encyclopedia of Textiles*, New York, 1958, pl. 15a
Complementary-weft weave with three-span floats in alternating alignment with 2/2 vertical color changes; alternating single and paired warps
Warp: undyed wool
Weft: undyed, red and green wool
Pile: undyed wool
51¼" x 17" (130.2 cm x 43.2 cm)
Acquired in 1950 from Phocion Tano, Cairo
31.12

111 Fragment with a geometric pattern
Fifth century

Textiles in the Louvre and in the Metropolitan Museum of Art have closely similar patterns (du Bourguet: *Catalogue des étoffes coptes*, no. G3; Dimand, "Early Christian Weavings from Egypt," fig. 3). The pattern may be derived from the floral quatrefoils that were often used in tapestries (Wulff and Volbach: *Spätantike und koptische Stoffe*, no. 9005, pl. 65 and no. 9112, pl. 78; Shurinova: *Coptic Textiles*, no. 105; Egger: *Koptische Textilien*, pl. 22).

Complementary-weft weave with three-span floats in alternating alignment with 2/2 vertical color changes; alternating single and paired warps
Warp: undyed wool
Weft: undyed, purple and black wool
13¼" x 12¼" (33.6 cm x 31.1 cm)
Acquired in 1951 from Phocion Tano, Cairo
31.14

112 Silk fragment with a diagonal grid pattern

Sixth century

The design of this textile closely resembles that of cat. no. 113. For another example of the grid pattern in silk see von Falke: *Kunstgeschichte der Seidenweberei*, vol. I, pl. 34. A tapestry at Dumbarton Oaks, no. 46.16, is similar in style; see Weibel: *Two Thousand Years of Textiles*, pl. 5. The palmette is similar to those appearing in one of the most important Early Byzantine medallion silks, now in the Vatican; see von Falke, I, pl. 68.

Complementary-weft weave with five-span floats in diagonal alignment; the three colors not appearing on the front are carried parallel on the back.
Warp: brown silk
Weft: red, green, blue and cream-colored silk
Extreme dimensions: 9⅝" x 8½" (24.5 cm x 21.6 cm)
Acquired in 1948 from James Pullen, Oakland
11.11

113 Silk fragment with a diagonal grid pattern

Sixth century

For the stylistic affiliations of this silk see cat. no. 112.

Complementary-weft weave with five-span floats in diagonal alignment; the color not appearing on the front is carried parallel on the back.
Warp: tan silk
Weft: red, green and cream-colored silk
6⅛" x 3⅜" (16 cm x 9 cm)
Acquired in 1948 from James Pullen, Oakland
11.12

114 Silk fragment with birds in a diagonal floral grid
Sixth century

Several other fragments of the same silk survive; see for example Weibel: *Two Thousand Years of Textiles*, pl. 52, and Errera: *Collection d'anciennes étoffes égyptiennes*, no. 220. Other pieces in similar style include Kendrick: *Catalogue of Textiles*, vol. III, pls. 31 and 32. For a much more elaborate treatment of the same theme see E. Vogt, "Frühmittelalterliche Stoffe aus der Abtei St. Maurice," *Zeitschrift für schweizerige Archäologie und Kunstgeschichte*, 18 (1958), pp. 110-140, pl. 35. The floral grid pattern was widely imitated in tapestry: cf. Akashi: *Coptic Textiles*, vol. III, pl. 104; Errera, nos. 222 and 223; Wulff and Volbach: *Spätantike und koptische Stoffe*, nos. 9585 and 9615, pl. 117.
Complementary-weft weave with five-span floats in diagonal alignment
Warp: cream-colored silk
Weft: red silk, cream-colored silk
12¼" x 10" (33.5 cm x 25.5 cm)
Acquired in 1949 from Paul Mallon, Paris
11.21

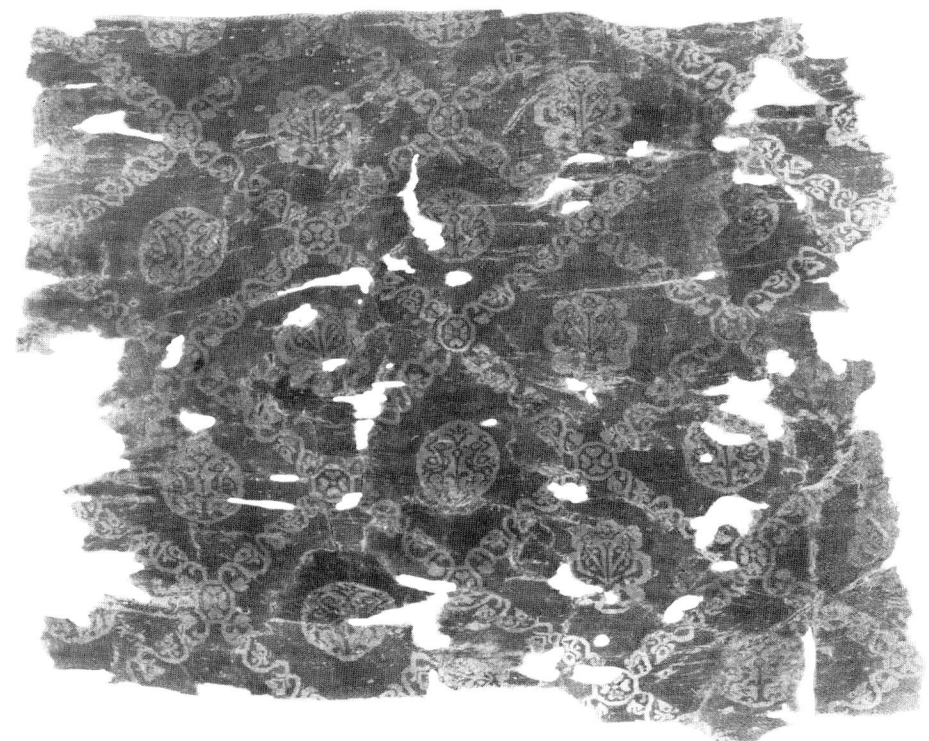

115 Silk fragment with men and tigers in combat
Late sixth or early seventh century
This textile was originally part of a pattern consisting of many identical circular medallions placed close together and containing either identical figures or two sets of figures in alternation. For stylistically related pieces and a discussion of the dating of the group, see Peirce and Tyler: *l'Art byzantin*, vol. II, 197b-e.
Complementary-weft weave with five-span floats in diagonal alignment
Warp: cream-colored silk
Weft: red silk, cream-colored silk
6¼" x 6⅛" (16 cm x 15 cm)
Acquired in 1950 from Phocion Tano, Cairo
11.26

RESIST-DYED TEXTILES

Tapestries, weft-loop textiles, and drawloom textiles, however much they may differ in technique and appearance, are alike in one fundamental way. In each case the creation of the pattern is inseparable from the weaving of the fabric itself. The two textiles illustrated here represent an entirely different approach to decoration. In resist-dyeing, as practiced in Late Antiquity, designs were painted onto already-woven, undyed linen, using a combination of a resist (a substance impervious to dye, e.g. wax) and a mordant (a substance which fixes the color of a dye). The entire cloth was then immersed in dye, almost invariably indigo, which affected it only where the mordant had been applied. When the resist was removed, the pattern appeared drawn in blue and in the natural color of the linen, against a blue background.

The technique of resist-dyeing, which seems to have been an Egyptian specialty, lent itself to elaborate figural compositions of great freedom and energy. (For the most spectacular of these, a Dionysiac scene now in the Louvre, see R. Bianchi-Bandinelli: *Rome: The Late Empire*, New York, 1971, pl. 45.) Much attention was lavished on details of costume and ornament, but the overriding impression remains one of spontaneity.

Christian scenes outnumber pagan ones in the surviving resist-dyed textiles. However, there is no stylistic distinction between pagan and Christian examples, and given the poor condition of many of the textiles it is not always possible to say with certainty what subject is depicted.

A concise account of Late Antique resist-dyed textiles appears in Kendrick: *Catalogue of Textiles*, vol. III, pp. 60ff. See also V. Illgen: *Zweifarbige reservetechnisch eingefärbte Leinenstoffe mit grossfigurigen biblischen Darstellungen aus Ägypten* (doctoral dissertation, Johannes Gutenberg-Universität, Mainz), Mainz, 1968.

◀ **116 Fragment depicting the infancy of Dionysus (?)**
Fourth or fifth century

The fragmentary condition of this textile makes its subject difficult to identify with certainty, but cf. the scenes from the life of Dionysus in the upper register of the resist-dyed textile in the Louvre, cited in the introduction to this section.

Resist-dyed linen, plain weave
Maximum dimensions: 22″ x 17½″ (55.9 cm x 44.5 cm)
Acquired in 1950 from Phocion Tano, Cairo
72.178A

117 Two fragments depicting a standing figure
Fourth or fifth century

The reconstruction seen here is conjectural, as the two fragments may not be from the same composition. Because the context is lost and the Greek inscription is too fragmentary to be read, it has not been possible to identify the figure.

Resist-dyed linen, plain weave
Upper fragment: 16½″ x 10¼″ (42 cm x 26 cm); lower fragment: 11½″ x 10½″ (29.2 cm x 26.7 cm)
Acquired in 1950 from Phocion Tano, Cairo
72.178B

APPENDIX I

THE DEVELOPMENT OF INTERLACE AND RELATED PATTERNS

The term "interlace" refers to patterns composed of bands which seem to pass over and under one another, creating the illusion of a third dimension.[1] Together with simpler but stylistically related geometric patterns, interlace plays an important role in Late Roman decorative art, including tapestry. However, this aspect of Roman art has largely been neglected by art historians, and is almost unknown to the general public. This may seem surprising, since late Roman ornament was an important source both for Islamic art and for the art of early medieval Europe.[2] Why, when these styles are widely enjoyed, does Roman interlace and geometric ornament receive so little attention? The probable reason is that Islam and Dark Age Europe are known to have placed, each for its own reasons, an overwhelming emphasis on non-figural patterns. In contrast, Roman art is the representational art *par excellence,* with naturalistic representation pervading even the so-called minor arts. It is therefore understandable that a non-representational form of decoration such as interlace, which seems to run counter to everything that Roman art stands for, should be seen as peripheral and fail to receive the attention it deserves. Without devaluing the figural tradition, an appreciation of interlace and geometric ornament can enrich our understanding of Late Roman art, reminding us not only of its variety but of the extent to which it anticipated and engendered the art of the very different cultures which succeeded the Roman Empire in Europe and Western Asia.

Tapestries with interlace and related patterns were executed primarily in purple. Although precise dating is impossible, by far the greatest proportion of interlace-patterned tapestries appear to have been made between ca. A.D. 300 and some time in the sixth century. To refine the chronology further it is necessary to rely on the evidence of an extremely small number of datable examples. Gradually working outward from these, one may begin to fill the gaps from the very large number of surviving undated pieces. The obvious danger of this method is that it means basing one's conclusions about the entire textile production of a period on a single example which may or may not be truly representative of that period. How accurately did the textile express the taste of its time? Was it conservative or innovative? Did it owe its existence to a widespread fashion or to a local workshop tradition? In the present state of knowledge these questions cannot be answered; therefore only the most tentative chronology is possible.

The dating of geometric and interlace tapestries depends above all on two fragments.[3] One comes from Palmyra in Syria and must date from before the city's destruction in

---

1. The design term "interlace" as used in this catalogue should not be confused with the textile structure term "interlacing," which is defined by Irene Emery as "the most straightforward way of interworking elements, inasmuch as each element simply passes under or over elements that cross its path" (Emery: *The Primary Structures of Fabrics,* p. 62). The close kinship between the two terms is obvious, but "interlace" refers only to a type of pattern, not to a fabric structure.

2. For early Islamic interlace see K.A.C. Creswell: *Early Muslim Architecture,* vols. 1 (2nd ed. in 2 vols.), Oxford, 1969, and 2, Oxford, 1940; R.W. Hamilton; *Khirbat al-Mafjar,* Oxford, 1959. For Western Medieval interlace and its relation to the Late Roman tradition, see N. Åberg: *The Occident and the Orient in the Art of the Seventh Century,* 3 vols., Stockholm, 1945.

3. I omit from my discussion two textiles widely accepted as dated. They were found at Hawara in Egypt by W.M. Flinders Petrie and reproduced in his *Hawara, Biahmu and Arsinoé,* London, 1889, pl. 21. Petrie states that they are datable ca. 340 by a coin of a son of the emperor Constantine which was found with them. While this statement may be correct, it is now incapable of being either proved or disproved. The coin is not reproduced in Petrie's publication, and Dr. Geoffrey T. Martin of the Petrie Collection, University College London, informs me that there is no way of identifying it among the many coins from Hawara in the Collection, or for that matter of knowing if it is there at all, since the exact find-spots of the coins are not recorded. I have been unable to discover the present location of the textiles.

Fig. 1. Tapestry fragment from a tunic, from Palmyra, Syria. Roman, before 273. After Pfister: *Textiles de Palmyre*.

A.D. 273 (fig. 1). The other was found at Karanis in Egypt, and must have been made before ca. A.D. 460, when that city was abandoned (fig. 2).[4] The most superficial comparison of these two textiles points to an evolution from simple to complex forms, and further evidence supports this view, although of course the actual development is much more complicated.

An Egyptian painted funerary portrait now in the Vatican shows the deceased in a shroud decorated with tapestry roundels virtually identical to the one from Palmyra.[5] The portrait has been independently dated on the basis of style to the third century, reinforcing the conjecture that the pattern of interlocking squares is not only the simplest type of

---

4. Pfister: *Textiles de Palmyre*, pl. 6; Wilson: *Ancient Textiles from Egypt*, no. 79, pl. 6.

5. Guimet: *Les portraits d'Antinoë*, pl. 46, fig. 72. For a recent discussion of the date see K. Parlasca: *Mumienporträts und verwandte Denkmäler*, Wiesbaden, 1966, pp. 138ff.

Fig. 2. Tapestry roundel with interlace ornament, from Karanis, Egypt. Late Roman, before ca. 460. Kelsey Museum of Archaeology, University of Michigan.

Fig. 3. Tapestry roundel with simple interlace ornament. Late Roman, here attributed to the early fourth century. The Metropolitan Museum of Art, New York, no. 89.18.176, purchase.

interlace but also the earliest. Another very early stage is represented by a tapestry roundel in the Metropolitan Museum of Art (fig. 3).[6] A garment in a lost fresco from Luxor, Egypt, dating from ca. 300, bore what seems to have been a very similar design.[7] Unfortunately the only record we have of this fresco is a watercolor copy made when it was already much deteriorated, so it is impossible to be completely sure of the pattern. Nevertheless, even without this corroborating evidence the simplicity of the motif in fig. 3 places it, with the Palmyra tapestry, at or near the very beginning of the development of interlace.

The tapestry shown in fig. 3 is important not just as an example of interlace in its formative stage; it tells us much about the interrelation of patterns in Roman decorative art, and the ways in which one might evolve into another. The simple interlace pattern of this textile is superimposed on a cruciform arrangement of lozenges with inward-curving sides. By first thickening the sides of the lozenges, and then interlacing them with the foreground motif, one arrives at the pattern used on a textile in the Textile Museum (cat. no. 82).[8] Alternatively, by using only the lozenges, increasing their number and accentuating the curvilinear element, it is possible to create a pattern of circles which may be seen in its most sophisticated form in another of the Textile Museum's examples (cat. no. 98).[9]

The movement away from the initial simplicity of figs. 1 and 3 which these two works illustrate is characteristic of the development of interlace in general. Thus cat. nos. 82 and 98 display a degree of confidence and elaboration inconceivable without the passage of time. Exactly how much time is impossible to determine, but it is fair to assume that they date from some time in the first half of the fourth century. The tendency toward greater complexity—and in most cases toward greater suppleness as well—is reflected in a number of examples from other collections.[10] However, the finest example of this period may well be cat. no. 83, which represents a slightly later stage of development, perhaps the mid to late fourth century. Although its pattern is complex it does not seem so, being balanced almost perfectly by precision and clarity of execution. This equilibrium is not typical and in later works the trend toward greater and greater elaboration is accelerated with a consequent loss of clarity. A tapestry in the Metropolitan Museum (fig. 4) shows the virtuosity of which weavers were capable around

---

6. Unpublished; Met. Mus. no. 89.18.176.

7. U. Monneret de Villard: "The Temple of the Imperial Cult at Luxor," *Archaeologia*, 95 (1953), pp. 85-105 and pl. 31a.

8. The transition is illustrated by three tapestry roundels in European museums. See Apostolakis: *Ta Koptika Huphasmata*, fig. 10; Kendrick: *Catalogue of Textiles*, vol. I, no. 187, pl. 27; du Bourguet: *Catalogue des étoffes coptes*, no. B6.

9. For intermediate stages in this development see du Bourguet: *Catalogue des étoffes coptes*, nos. B1 and C59.

10. See for example Akashi: *Coptic Textiles*, vol. I, pl. 2 and vol. II, pl. 74; Renner: "Spätantike figürliche Pupurwirkereien," figs. 1 and 2.

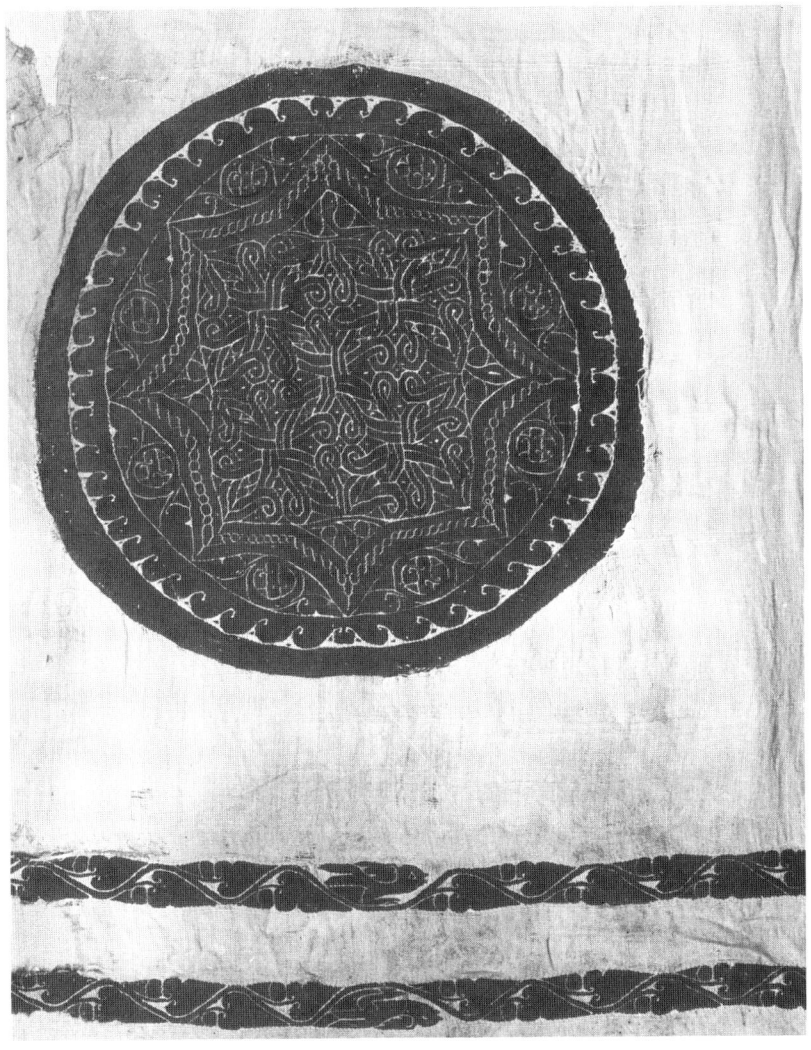

Fig. 4. Tapestry roundel with complex interlace ornament. Late Roman, here attributed to the late fourth or early fifth century. The Metropolitan Museum of Art, New York, no. 89.18.151, purchase.

the end of the fourth century or the beginning of the fifth.[11] Cat. no. 84 probably represents the same phase, though a narrow border naturally provides far less scope for elaboration than does a roundel.

This combination of intricacy and suppleness was evidently beyond the power of many artists, or else tastes simply altered. In any case, although patterns remain complex their appearance changes. The drawing becomes stiffer and more geometric, curves lost their fluidity. There is also a tendency to conceive the pattern no longer as an indivisible large unit, but as an assembly of smaller ones. Cat. no. 85 illustrates this tendency, which is even more pronounced—note the change from curves, even abrupt ones, to sharp points—in the Karanis tapestry (fig. 2) which as we have seen dates from before ca. 460.[12] Cat. no. 85 can therefore probably be dated to the early to middle fifth century.

---

11. Met. Mus. no. 89.18.151; see Kajitani, "Coptic Fragments," no. 13, p. 13.
12. For other examples of the same style see Lewis: *Early Coptic Textiles*, pls. 24 and 25; Peter: *Textilien aus Ägypten*, no. 115. Especially instructive is the comparison of cat. no. 84 with a border of the later type, in the Louvre (du Bourguet: *Catalogue des étoffes coptes*, no. B33).

The dating of the later, geometrized phase of interlace, exemplified by the Karanis piece, to the mid-fifth century makes it possible to date a number of closely related tapestries as well. A tapestry square in the Metropolitan Museum (fig. 5)[13] includes, in addition to interlace of the Karanis type, four small squares each of which contains four interlaced circles. They are of a different kind from any interlace we have considered so far. Lacking the complexity and sense of motion of earlier forms, the new interlace has a tentativeness of articulation that is very different from the flamboyant abruptness of the "Karanis-style" interlace with which it is juxtaposed. A less fundamental feature, but still a distinguishing one, is the use of cross-hatching on the bands.

Since the arrangement of four interlaced circles is found almost unchanged at the center of the right half of cat. no. 86, we may assume that this tapestry too dates from around the middle of the fifth century. This is important because the motif that occupies the corresponding position in the left

---

13. Unpublished; Met. Mus. no. 90.5.880.

Fig. 5. Tapestry square with floral and interlace motifs. Late Roman, here attributed to the middle of the fifth century. The Metropolitan Museum of Art, New York, no. 90.5.880, gift of George F. Baker.

Fig. 6. Tapestry square with floral and interlace motifs. Late Roman, here attributed to the second half of the fifth century. The Metropolitan Museum of Art, New York, no. 89.18.252, purchase.

half of the design—an eight-pointed star containing a simple two-band interlace with cross-hatching—is found in four other tapestries in the Textile Museum's collection: cat. nos. 87-90. It is therefore likely that they too date from the mid-fifth century. This group, then, does not represent a different historical phase from the "Karanis-style," but rather a different approach to the problem of decorating with interlace.

We are almost certainly looking at the production, or at least the influence, of two separate workshops or groups of workshops. This conclusion is borne out by an important technical consideration. Tapestries of the first group are woven on a linen warp, while those of the second group have warps of wool.

Although the tapestries of the second group which we have looked at so far are probably contemporary with the latest phase of the first group, other tapestries of the second type have features which point to a later date, in all likelihood the second half of the fifth century. Thus an example in the Metropolitan Museum (fig. 6)[14] has a central interlace motif which clearly belongs to the second group, but which is far more complex than any of that group which we have yet seen. The more loosely structured central interlace of cat. no. 91 is closely related, but whether it is of similar date or later is difficult to say.

Cat. no. 93 belongs to the same general interlace type, but in it the rather diffuse structure of no. 91 is replaced by a pattern whose precision and assurance barely compensate for a hardness bordering on monotony. In spirit if not in exact detail it corresponds to the treatment of interlace in sixth-century sculpture.[15] Certainly there is no reason to date it later than the sixth century, or even, perhaps, later than the middle of that century. A further group of tapestries, while artistically inferior to cat. no. 93, are closely related to it stylistically. Most important of these is cat. no. 92, but the group also includes cat. nos. 94 and 95. It is worth noting that in the last of these the interlace, while apparently complex, relies on simple loops and crossovers, implying a decline either in technical command or in the imaginative design sense that created and maintained the tradition of interlace ornament. Such a decline is confirmed by cat. no. 96; it is a close stylistic relation of the three works just mentioned, but its interlace is for the most part reduced to an unimaginative series of disconnected loops. This may be said to mark the effective end of interlace as a theme in Late Roman textile design, probably around the end of the sixth century.

The varied history of interlace, the rise and fall of distinct stylistic groups within it, and especially the evidence for its decline in the sixth century, all suggest that its final extinction is part of the internal history of Egyptian textile manufacture—assuming that the tapestries were woven in Egypt—rather than an effect of the Muslim conquests of the early seventh century. In other media, notably sculpture and metalwork, interlace continued for centuries to play an essential role in both Christian and Muslim art throughout Europe and much of Asia.

---

14. Unpublished; Met. Mus. no. 89.18.252.

15. For sixth-century architectural sculpture from Bawit in Egypt see E. Chassinat: *Fouilles à Baouit*, vol. I, Cairo, 1911, pl. 80. On the dating of the carvings see H. Torp: "The Carved Decorations of the North and South Churches at Bawit," *Kolloquium über spätantike und frühmittelalterliche Skulptur*, vol. II, Mainz, 1970, pp. 35-41.

APPENDIX II

REMOUNTING OF THE TAPESTRY CAT. NO. 1

by KATRINA DE CARBONNEL

The tapestry was remounted in the winter of 1981. Nearly eleven feet high and six feet wide (130 inches high and 72½ inches wide as mounted), it is so finely woven that one cannot detect which is the front and which is the back. No messy threads occur on what one might guess to be the reverse as is usually found on all European tapestries of a similar size. The colors still have a vigorous freshness and are bright on both the face and reverse of the textile as it is currently mounted. There is minimal fading. It is truly a double sided hanging.

When first mounted at the Textile Museum some twenty years ago the tapestry was sewn down with thousands of stitches of beige and red cotton thread on a red twill weave wool fabric especially dyed red to match the vivid red background of the tapestry itself.

The red support fabric was stretched over a heavy wooden strainer; the back of the mounted textile was protected by a peg board; and the whole package was framed behind thick plate glass, thereby creating a heavy and cumbersome mount. After an accident several years ago in which the protective glass broke and slashed a section of the red mounting fragment, it became essential to remount the tapestry. It seemed desirable to substitute in place of the red background, one of more neutral color, and in addition to devise a more manageable system of mounting.

The Director of the Textile Museum, Andrew Oliver, Jr., made arrangements with Joseph Columbus, Textile Conservator for the National Gallery of Art, Washington, D.C. for me to remount the tapestry at the National Gallery. I was provided with space and excellent lighting as well as the expert advise and help of Mr. Columbus and his assistant, Julie Woodward.

We considered it easier to unmount the textile by dividing it into sections of manageable size. The textile was therefore placed face up on a large table and sections were cut out of the old mounting fabric around the islands of fragments of the original textile. Quarter inch foamcore was slid under each section of mounted textile. Thick Mylar sheets were placed on top of each section and another sheet of foamcore was placed on top of this. The edges of each sandwich thus formed were taped and straight pins inserted at five inch intervals to keep the layers from sliding. Flipping the packaged section of textile over and placing it face down on the working table the pins were removed and edges untaped. With the foamcore removed the reverse of the mounted textile was thus exposed and the stitches and knots holding the fragments to the mount were individually clipped and pulled out with tweezers.

Splinters of broken glass were found lodged in and behind the textile and a few dead silverfish were discovered near where they had eaten small holes in the red mounting fabric. It was also noticed that the red mounting fabric had faded where not hidden behind the fragments mounted on it. Once all the stitches were pulled out the mounting material was gently rolled off the original textile revealing the reverse of the tapestry.

A thick plain weave cotton of neutral brown color was chosen as a mounting support to replace the red one. The new cloth was hand washed in Orvus, well rinsed and ironed and then cut in three pieces and machine sewed to form a backing of the proper size and shape. The seams were calculated to be hidden as much as possible under fragments of the original textile. The mounting fabric was stretched with push pins over a strong but light bass wood strainer equipped with two removable cross bars. To insure proper tension it was restretched after two days and then the edges were stretched over the back of the strainer and stapled down. The push pins were then removed.

After each section of tapestry was unmounted it was covered with a layer of thick Mylar topped by a quarter inch sheet of foamcore. These sandwiches were then once again pinned, taped and flipped over. The foamcore (then on top) was removed and the fragments shifted on to the new brown mounting material. Using photographs of the textile as it had been previously mounted, the various sections were correctly positioned. A few minor adjustments were made to improve the alignment.

The foamcore sheets were slid out from under the fragments and after the final positioning the Mylar sheets were slid out as well. The fragments were sewn down with brown cotton thread. A straight needle was used when practical and a curved needle for all the other areas.

The newly mounted textile has now been framed behind quarter inch ultraviolet absorbing plexiglas to prevent further deterioration or accidents.

The weft is made up of nineteen colors of wool and a few tiny spots of white linen (see note). These colored wools are woven together on a natural colored wool warp with such skill that I feel the weaver must have faithfully copied from a painted cartoon. Old repairs indicated that the tapestry saw considerable use as a curtain or hanging.

Note: Colors found in weft of tapestry coded using the Munsell color charts with mask B.

This list can be used as a reference to check for possible future fading of the textile.

1. red (background)   Red 4/8
2. dark purple (shadow of cape figure lower right)   Purplish Red 3/4
3. medium purple (second shading or same cape)   Purplish Red 3/8
4. pink (lightest shading of same cape)   Red 6/6
5. mustard (lower decorative bands)   Reddish Yellow 7/6
6. yellow (lower decorative bands with birds and fruits)   Yellow 7/6
7. dark green (leaves in lower border)   Green 4/4
8. light green (circular bands of stems in lower border)   Yellowish Green Yellow 7/4
9. lightest flesh tone   Yellow 8/4
10. second flesh tone   Yellow 7/4
11. pinkish flesh tone   Reddish Yellow Red 7/4
12. medium green (cape 2nd figure from lower right)   Yellowish Green Yellow 6/4
13. dark blue (peacock body)   Purplish Blue 3/4
14. medium blue (peacock body)   Blueish Blue Green 6/2
15. light blue (peacock body)   Blueish Blue Green 7/2
16. lightest blue (cupid's wings figure lower right)   Blueish Blue Green 8/2
17. light brown (lower right figure's hair)   Reddish Yellow 5/4
18. orange (outline of peacock's back)   Yellow Red Yellow 6/6
19. black   Black n1/ 1.2%R

Table of Accession and Catalogue Numbers

Accession no.	Cat. no.	Accession no.	Cat. no.
1.48	20	71.106	30
11.11	112	71.107	31
11.12	113	71.108	32
11.21	114	71.112	105
11.26	115	71.113	85
11.27	15	71.114	79
31.11	108	71.115	80
31.12	110	71.117	25
31.14	111	71.118	1
71.4	16	71.119	68
71.5	12	71.120	76
71.6	53	71.121	69
71.10	3	71.122	57
71.14	17	71.123	62
71.16	50	71.124	58
71.18	2	71.126	100
71.19	36	71.128	40
71.24	72	71.132	4
71.26	37	71.133	54
71.31	86	711.8	74
71.32	70	711.15	78
71.33	18	711.18	93
71.34	98	711.26	45
71.38	55	711.30	46
71.42	102	711.40	6
71.43	71	72.30	33
71.45	104	72.32	60
71.46	106	72.35	96
71.47	13	72.61	23
71.48	103	72.63	61
71.49	67	72.64	59
71.51	19	72.72	92
71.53	88	72.79	75
71.58	87	72.90	24
71.60	48	72.103	11
71.61	52	72.121	7
71.62	51	72.124	43
71.63	10	72.126	38
71.67	49	72.128	8
71.71	39	72.132	56
71.72	26	72.136	28
71.73	66	72.145	29
71.78	14	72.151	95
71.79	42	72.153	99
71.80	5	72.165	9
71.81	77	72.178a	116
71.84	41	72.178b	117
71.87	64	72.183	22
71.90	21	1960.5.1	107
71.91	83	1960.20.7	47
71.92	81	1961.22.29a-e	27
71.94	91	1964.16.5	65
71.96	89	1964.17.1	94
71.97	97	1968.8.8	34
71.98	73	no number	109
71.99	101		
71.100	44		
71.101	63		
71.102	35		
71.103	84		
71.104	82		
71.105	90		

BIBLIOGRAPHY

This bibliography includes works on many aspects of Late Roman and Early Byzantine textile art. Nevertheless, it is not intended to be exhaustive. Works marked with an asterisk (*) are, in the author's opinion, of special importance for their comprehensiveness, for the quality of the material they present, or for their contribution to textile history.

Age of Spirituality. Edited by K. Weitzmann. Metropolitan Museum of Art, New York, 1979.

K. Akashi, *Coptic Textiles from the Burying Grounds in Egypt in the Collection of the Kanegafuchi Spinning Company*, 3 vols., Kyoto, 1955.

A. Apostolakis, *Ta Koptika Huphasmata tou an Athēnais Mouseiou Kosmetikōn Technōn*, Athens, 1932.

*S.M. Arensberg, "Dionysos: A Late Antique Tapestry," *Boston Museum Bulletin*, 75 (1977), pp. 4-25.

L'Art copte. Petit Palais, Paris, 1964.

A. Baginski and A. Tidhar. *Textiles from Egypt, 4th-13th Centuries C.E.* L.A. Mayer Memorial Institute for Islamic Art, Jerusalem, 1980.

J. Beckwith, "Coptic Textiles," *CIBA Review*, 12,133 (1959), pp. 2-27.

L. Bellinger, "Textile Analysis: Early Techniques in Egypt and the Near East" (pt. 3), *Textile Museum Workshop Notes*, Paper no. 6, (November, 1952.)

R. Berliner, "A Coptic Tapestry of Byzantine Style," *Textile Museum Journal*, 1,1 (1962), pp. 3-22.

———, "Remarks on Some Tapestries from Egypt," *Textile Museum Journal*, 1,4, (1965), pp. 20-41.

E. Billeter, *Aussereuropäische Textilien*. Kunstgewerbemuseum, Zürich, 1963.

G.M. Crowfoot and J. Griffiths, "Coptic Textiles in Two-Faced Weave with Pattern in Reverse," *Journal of Egyptian Archaeology*, 25 (1939), pp. 40-47.

M.S. Dimand, *Die Ornamentik der ägyptischen Wollwirkereien*. Leipzig, 1924

———, "Early Christian Weavings from Egypt," *Bulletin of the Metropolitan Museum of Art*, 20 (1925), pp. 55-58.

———, "Coptic Tunics in the Metropolitan Museum," *Metropolitan Museum Studies*, 2, pt. 2 (1930), pp. 239-252.

———, "An Early Cut-Pile Rug from Egypt," *Metropolitan Museum Studies*, 4, pt. 2 (1953), pp. 151-162.

———, "Coptic and Egypto-Arabic Textiles," *Bulletin of the Metropolitan Museum of Art*, 26 (1939), pp 89-91.

*———, "Classification of Coptic Textiles," in *Coptic Egypt* (Papers read at a symposium held under the joint auspices of New York University and the Brooklyn Museum, in connection with the exhibition "Pagan and Christian Egypt"), Brooklyn, 1944, pp. 51-58.

P. du Bourguet, "La datation des tissus coptes," *Bulletin de la Société française d'Égyptologie*, 13 (1953), pp. 60-67.

———, "Datation des tissus coptes en fonction des mosaiques mediterranéennes," *Ars Orientalis*, 3 (1959), pp. 189-192.

*———, *Musée national du Louvre. Catalogue des étoffes coptes*. Paris, 1964.

G. Egger, *Koptische Textilien*. Österreichisches Museum für angewandte Kunst, Vienna, 1967.

*I. Emery, *The Primary Structures of Fabrics*. The Textile Museum, Washington, D.C., 1966 (2nd ed., 1980).

*I. Errera, *Collection d'anciennes etoffes égyptiennes*, Brussels, 1916.

*O. von Falke, *Kunstegeschichte der Seidenweberei*, 2 vols., Berlin, 1913.

———, *Decorative Silks*, New York, 1936.

J.F. Flanagan, "The Origin of the Drawloom Used in the Making of Early Byzantine Silks," *The Burlington Magazine*, 35 (1919), pp. 167-172.

R. Forrer, *Römische und byzantinische Seiden-Textilien aus dem Gräberfelde von Achmim-Panopolis*, Strassburg, 1891.

G. de Francovich, "L'Egitto, la Siria, Costantinopoli: problemi di metodo," *Rivista dell' Istituto Nazionale d'Archeologia e Storia dell' Arte*, 11-12 (1968), pp. 83-229.

Frühchristliche und koptische Kunst. Akademie der bildende Künste, Vienna, 1964.

* A. Geijer, "A Silk from Antinoë and the Sassanian Textile Art," *Orientalia Suecana*, 12 (1963), pp. 3-36.

———, "The Viminacium Gold Tapestry," *Meddelanden fran Lunds Universitets Historiska Museum*, 1964-65, pp. 223-236.

———, *A History of Textile Art*, London, 1969.

V. Gervers, ed., *Studies in Textile History in Memory of Harold B. Burnham*. Royal Ontario Museum, Toronto, 1977.

L. Guerrini, *Le stoffe copte del Museo Archeologico di Firenze*, Rome, 1957.

E. Guimet, *Les Portraits d'Antinoë au Musée Guimet*, Paris, 1912.

V. Illgen, *Zweifarbige reservetechnisch eingefärbte Leinenstoffe mit grossfigurigen biblischen Darstellungen aus Ägypten* (doctoral dissertation, Johannes Gutenberg-Universität), Mainz, 1968.

R. Jaques and E. Flemming, *Encyclopedia of Textiles*, New York, 1958.

*N. Kajitani, "Coptic Fragments" (in Japanese), *Textile Art* (Kyoto), 13 (1981), pp., 6-77.

*A.F. Kendrick, *Catalogue of Textiles from Burying Grounds in Egypt*. 3 vols. Victoria and Albert Museum, London, 1920-22.

*____, "Early Textiles in the Canton Valais," *Burlington Magazine*, 45 (1924), pp. 125-131.

*E. Kitzinger, "The Horse and Lion Tapestry at Dumbarton Oaks: A Study in Coptic and Sassanian Textile Design," *Dumbarton Oaks Papers*, 3 (1946), pp. 1-72.

**Koptische Kunst: Christentum am Nil*. Villa Hügel, Essen, Essen-Bredeney, 1963.

Koptische Kunst: Christentum am Nil. Kunsthaus, Zürich, 1964.

*L. Kybalova, *Coptic Textiles*, London, 1967.

C.J. Lamm and R.J. Charleston, "Some Early Egyptian Drawloom Weavings," *Bulletin de la Société d'Archéologie Copte*, 5 (1939).

M. Lemberg and B. Schmedding. *Abegg-Stiftung Bern in Riggisberg. II. Textilien*. Schweizer Heimatbücher, 17 (3-4). Bern, 1973.

V. Lenzen, "The Triumph of Dionysos on Textiles of Late Antique Egypt," *University of California Publications in Classical Archaeology*, 5 (1960), pp. 1-38.

S. Lewis, *Early Coptic Textiles*, Stanford, 1969.

____, "The Iconography of the Coptic Horseman in Byzantine Egypt," *Journal of the American Research Center in Egypt*, 10 (1973), pp. 27-64.

C. Lubell, *Textile Collections of the World*, 3 vols., New York, 1976-77.

M. Matie (Matthieu) and K. Liapunova, *Textiles of Coptic Egypt* (in Russian), Leningrad, 1951.

C.C. Mayer-Thurman and B. Williams, *Ancient Textiles from Nubia*, Chicago, 1979.

Pagan and Christian Egypt. Brooklyn Museum, Brooklyn, 1941.

K. Parlasca, *Mumienporträts und verwandte Denkmäler*. Wiesbaden, 1966.

*H. Peirce and R. Tyler. *L'Art byzantin*, 2 vols., Paris, 1932-34.

I. Peter, *Textilien aus Ägypten im Museum Rietberg Zürich*, Zürich, 1976.

*R. Pfister, "La decoration des étoffes d'Antinoë," *Revue des arts asiatiques*, 5 (1928), pp. 215-243.

____, "Les debuts du vêtement copte," *Etudes d'Orientalisme publiées par le Musée Guimet à la mémoire du Raymonde Linoissier*, Paris, 1932.

____, *Textiles de Palmyre*, Paris, 1934.

*____, "Le rôle de l'Iran dans les textiles d'Antinoë," *Ars Islamica*, 13-14 (1948), pp. 46-74.

M.-Th. Picard-Schmitter, "Une tapisserie hellenistique d'Antinoë, au Musée du Louvre," *Monuments Piot* (Académie des inscriptions et belles-lettres, Paris. Commission de la fondation Piot. *Monuments et mémoires*), 52 (1962), pp. 27-35.

M. Reinhold, *History of Purple as a Status Symbol in Antiquity*, Brussels, 1970.

D. Renner, *Die koptischen Stoffe im Martin von Wagner Museum der Universität Würzburg*, Weisbaden, 1974.

*____, "Spätantike figurliche Purpurwirkerien," in *Documenta Textilia: Festschrift für Sigrid Müller-Christensen*, edited by M. Flury-Lemberg and K. Stollers, Munich, 1981, pp. 82-94.

*H. Seyrig and L. Robert. "Sur un tissu récemment publié," *Cahiers Archéologiques*, 8 (1956), pp. 27-36.

*D. Shepherd, "An Icon of the Virgin: A Sixth-Century Tapestry Panel from Egypt," *Bulletin of the Cleveland Museum of Art*, 56, 3 (1969), pp. 90-120.

*R. Shurinova, *Coptic Textiles: Collection of Coptic Textiles, State Pushkin Museum of Fine Arts, Moscow*, Moscow, 1967.

D. Thompson, *Coptic Textiles in the Brooklyn Museum*, Brooklyn, 1971.

N.P. Toll, *Coptic Textiles of the Art-Industrial Museum in Prague* (in Russian), Prague, 1928.

E. Vogt, "Frühmittelalterliche Stoffe aus der Abtei St. Maurice," *Zeitschrift für schweizerige Archäologie und Kunstgeschichte*, 18 (1958), pp. 111-140.

W.F. Volbach, *Spätantike und Frühmittelalterliche Stoffe*. Römisch-Germanisches Zentralmuseum, Mainz, 1932.

____, *Early Decorative Textiles*, London and New York, 1969.

A.J.B. Wace, "Preliminary Historical Study: A Late Roman Tapestry from Egypt," *Textile Museum Workshop Notes*, Paper no. 9 (1954.)

A.C. Weibel, *Two Thousand Years of Tapestry Weaving*, Hartford, 1951.

*____, *Two Thousand Years of Textiles*, New York, 1952.

K. Wessel, *Coptic Art in Early Christian Egypt*, New York, 1965.

L. Wilson, *Ancient Textiles from Egypt in the University of Michigan Collection*, Ann Arbor, 1933.

E. Wipszycka, *L'Industrie textile dans l'Egypte romaine*, Wroclaw, 1965.

*O. Wulff and W.F. Volbach, *Spätantike und koptische Stoffe aus ägyptischen Grabfunden in den Staatlichen Museen*, Berlin, 1926.

H. Zaloscer, *Ägyptische Wirkereien*, Bern, 1962.